The Moment I Decided to *OWN It*

TANYA ARMSTRONG

Copyright © 2017 by Tanya R. Armstrong. All rights reserved.

All content is copyrighted by OWN It Publishing. No part, either text or image, may be used for any purpose other than personal use. Reproduction, modification, storage in a retrieval system or retransmission, in any form or by any means, electronic, mechanical, or otherwise, for reasons other than personal use, without prior written permission from the publisher is strictly prohibited.

Printed in the United States of America

ISBN: 978-0-692-37480-1

To my children

CONTENTS

INTRODUCTION: Move Your Feet 1

CHAPTER ONE: False Appearances 5

CHAPTER TWO: I Do 17

CHAPTER THREE: Betrayed 21

CHAPTER FOUR: Married, But Single 29

CHAPTER FIVE: New Addition 35

CHAPTER SIX: Are You Serious? (Twins) 41

CHAPTER SEVEN: Single Parent 49

CHAPTER EIGHT: He's Back! 57

CHAPTER NINE: DNR (Do Not Resuscitate) 65

CHAPTER TEN: Ho Ho Ho, Daddy No Mo 75

CHAPTER ELEVEN: I'm Lost 87

CHAPTER TWELVE: Digging Deep 95

CHAPTER THIRTEEN: The Aha Moment 101

INTRODUCTION:
MOVE YOUR FEET

YOU WAKE UP THINKING, *This must be a delusion, a nightmare,* and discover all of your life's plans destroyed, your dreams shattered. Never have you felt this alone. Trying to figure out how to take the next step when that next step is simply getting out of bed. Millions of thoughts flood your mind and you cannot make sense of any of it. Thinking, *How did it get to this place? Where did it all go so horrifically wrong? How will I survive this? When did Darren stop loving me? Did he ever love me? What could I have done differently? What is wrong with me? Will anyone ever love me? How will my children get past this? Did I fail them? Will they think it's my fault? Will I end up bitter? Will I ever trust again? Will I ever be able to forgive?*

On that late Wednesday evening in April after my dad had taken Darren back to the airport, the emotions of the day were beginning to crash down on me. Finally I became too tired to think and prepared to go to bed. I walked into the bedroom closet. As I was standing in my bathroom and looking at what used to be "his" side of the closet with tears streaming down my face, all these thoughts flooded my mind. The closet that used to seem so small at that moment seemed to be the biggest room in the house. My entire adult life with him was packed up in boxes labeled shoes, jeans, shirts, jackets, and watches. I did not know where I was going to draw the strength to breathe, much less to move my feet. He left me standing there alone to clean up the shattered pieces of not only my life but that of our children. All I could do was put my hands up on the wall to keep from falling.

"God, what am I going to do? How am I going to get past this? Why did he stop loving me? When did he become so indifferent about my heart? When did he stop seeing me?"

I should not be feeling this way because I was the one who filed the papers. I should feel free and happy about my decision but I felt far from that. I felt so alone!

He was going back to where his heart relocated, and I was standing in the place where my heart was broken. His heart served me an eviction notice and a new occupant now resided there. For Darren the 80/20 percent rule applied. While I was the woman who was the 80 percent, she was the woman who was the 20 percent that I could never be for him.

I was completely and utterly broken. I needed someone, anyone—even him—to hold me and whisper, "It's okay, I am here." But no one came, and again like many times in my life, I found myself alone. Alone to deal with my thoughts, alone to deal with my pain and my loss. I just wanted to close my eyes tight and open them to see my life fall back into place.

But when I opened them again, all that was looking back was loneliness.

April 3 started and I already knew that day would be the last time that he and I would ever share the same anything. I knew that would be that last time we would share space under the same roof, and that our story had reached its final chapter. That morning I got up, took my shower, and got dressed for work. I went into my daughter's room, where Darren was sitting watching television. I walked over to him, placed my hands on his shoulders, bent down, and kissed the top of his head.

I said, "I have always loved you ... " and then I turned around and walked out of the room.

The rest of that early morning we exchanged very few words. There was a great heaviness weighing on me. I knew what was going to take place later that morning. A part of me was like, *Yes! I hope this makes him feel the same kind of pain he has caused me.* Another part was second-guessing my decision. *Am I doing the right thing?*

I left for work hoping that I would hear from him, but when 9:45 a.m. came, I heard nothing. In my heart I just knew that he was going to call me at work and say, "I was wrong. Let's try to work this out."

That call never came, and even though I was hurting beyond belief, I knew I had made the right choice. At 6:15 a.m. on April 3, when I walked out of the house my marriage was effectively over. In that moment, Darren went from being my husband to my opponent.

CHAPTER ONE:
FALSE APPEARANCES

IT WAS A cool Friday afternoon in March 1994 that started like any other. I had made plans to hang out with my friend Tina at the University of Central Florida. My best friend Kim had invited us on campus to enjoy the final day of Greek week on campus. Kim was helping with some of the events and I decided to go and have some fun. Tina and I were walking around the campus, and that is where I laid eyes on Darren. I thought, *This man is fine!* We exchanged a few words in passing, and I continued hanging out with my girls. Sometime later that afternoon, I saw him again hanging out with some guys I knew. There was something about him that made me want to know him. Physically he had everything I wanted. He was average height but he was muscularly built, like a linebacker. He was five feet ten and 285 pounds of pure muscle. I was thinking to myself, *I have got to know him!* Wanting to meet him, I walked over and said hello to my friends. Before anyone could introduce us, Darren introduced himself to me and in his introduction he stated that he had seen me the night before at a talent show, but I left before he had an opportunity to speak. As he was talking to me all I kept thinking was, *Good gawd almighty, where do they make men like you, 'cause I have to go.* My first impression of him was he was charming; he had a beautiful smile, and his eyes—there was something about his eyes. I always said his appearance drew me in but his smile and those captivating eyes stole my heart. I remember that he had on a burgundy South Carolina Gamecocks sweatshirt, blue jeans, timberland boots, and a gray hat. He walked with a swagger and confidence that I was in awe of. Everything about him I wanted to know. I kept thinking, *This man is really fine!*

Our story started on that cool breezy but sunny Friday afternoon in March, around 2:30 p.m. We spoke several times a day; I practically lived in Darren's dormitory room. One would have thought I was a student at the university as often as I was there. I lived 45 minutes across town and at the time was attending a community college. I would take the hour-and-a-half city bus almost every day just to see him and many times would have to get a ride home or take the late bus back. Being around him was all I wanted to do. He won my heart with his smile, and I pondered if he could be the one. We started off being "special friends." We had no expectations of each other and we were free to date other people, but I never did.

All I really wanted was him.

I remember a time when I was hanging out in Darren's room, he went to take a shower, and a young lady came by the room looking for him. I told her that he was in the shower;

she said okay. Then I heard the shower door open. She pulled back the curtain and they proceeded to have a conversation. I assumed that was yet another young lady that he was seeing and immediately felt uncomfortable so I left. About an hour later I heard a knock on my friend's room door. I asked, "Who is at the door?" It was him, asking why I left the room. I said, "I thought you had company." Darren had explained that she was just a good friend, and I made myself believe it. I thought, *He came looking for me; he must care.* But my gut told me that he was lying.

Something was changing, and I remembered a conversation we had one night. We were just talking and he kept saying to me, "You know we are just friends, right?"

And I said, "Yes, I know because you are reminding me all the time."

Then he said, "I do that to remind myself because my feelings are starting to change."

I said nothing but deep inside I was shouting with excitement. All I ever wanted was for him to only want me and it was finally starting to happen. We continued dating and hanging out during the next several months. There was not a day that would go by without him and me seeing each other. There were times he would come to the house when my family and I were at church and leave a note in the mailbox for me to simply say he was thinking of me. Every note and every card made me feel as special as the words he would write in them. When he would come by my house to visit and spend time with not only me but my family I began to appreciate him for the man I thought he was. My mom thought the world of him at the time. She thought he was charming and handsome. She would give him gas money just for driving all the way to come see me and even cook dinner for him when he would come by. One warm Friday afternoon in early August, we had a huge argument over a conversation that Kim had with me. Kim called me around eleven that Friday morning and she stated that Darren had been seen with several women around campus and that a friend of hers came up to her to talk to her about it. She told Kim that she knew Darren was seeing me but I needed to be aware that he was seeing several other women at the same time and that on the nights I would leave campus from spending time with him another woman was coming by and staying the night. I became enraged not only at him but at myself for allowing myself to think that I was enough. We went at it toe to toe for several hours; we went back and forth. We argued from midafternoon until about 7:00 p.m. He drove all the way from the University of Central Florida to my parents' house, and we still argued. I had to get to choir rehearsal and he said that he was going to take me so that we could finish the argument. When we got to the church he said to me, "I am only fighting this hard because I love you and I'm not going to lose you over something that is not true."

That was it. He finally said what I wanted to hear, and nothing else mattered. Not even all the flags that were going off in my head. You see, when you are so desperate to have anyone love you, you will settle for anything that seems to be the perfect package.

THE MOMENT I DECIDED TO OWN IT

> Advice to my former self, my daughters, and to you, my readers: *Never doubt your gut! Listen to it because it is God's way of talking to you. You see, when you go against your gut feelings, you are setting yourself up. You are setting yourself up for heartbreak and pain! You are setting yourself up for a life of disappointment, and God is his infinite wisdom is trying to steer you away from the pain and the heartache you are headed toward. If it does not feel right; it is not right. When your head says to you, "Girl, hell no!" run like hell, baby—just run!*

We dated for almost a year, and we argued for most it. Many of the arguments were about other women that he would always say were just friends. There were times Darren thought I was in the bathroom taking a shower when I would hear him calling the operator to break into a telephone call so he could talk to the very woman we were arguing about. At times, I believed his roommate was trying to warn me by playing the voice messages from her to Darren when I would come to the apartment. The messages were always the same: "Where are you? What time are you coming by? I miss you. I love you."

And Darren would always say things to make her seem as if she was the crazy one and how she would not leave him alone. There was a phone call between this woman and one of my close friends where I was on mute listening to her. She told her when I would leave she would be in the apartment complex parking lot waiting so she could go in. She described his apartment and how the two of them were planning their future.

I told him what I heard, and he said it was not true because the times she gave were off. I convinced myself that she was lying. I was so afraid of being alone that I just held on to whatever lie he would tell me. Later that year, I found out I was pregnant with our first child. I will never forget that night.

Darren kept saying, "Something is wrong with you."

I had frequent headaches, was always tired, and I smelled the strangest things, so on a Wednesday night in March, we got the test.

I went to the bathroom in his apartment and urinated on the stick. We were looking at it because we lost the instructions and did not know what the two pink lines meant. I called a girlfriend, Trina, and she said, "Girl, I don't know. You better get another test."

Darren left and went to the store, which was approximately five minutes away from the apartment. Forty-five minutes passed, and he still had not returned. All sorts of thoughts ran through my mind. He left me. He's never coming back. I will be a statistic and worst of all a "baby momma." The door opened; he came back, but he looked a little different. His shoulders looked heavy and his face wore the look, *What are we going to do?* and he simply said, "I think you are pregnant." Still trying to convince not only himself but also me, he kept saying that maybe the test was wrong so he wanted to go to the family clinic. The next day we went to the local clinic, where they confirmed what the test said the night before—we were having a baby. In that moment, our lives changed and we had to grow up. This baby was coming, and life just became real.

THE MOMENT I DECIDED TO OWN IT

But the familiar thought *I am making a mistake* kept flooding my mind.

I was hoping that this would change him and he would settle down. The same warning flags were still there. Darren was not changing. There were still late phone calls from other women and whispering on the phone when he thought I was asleep. The "friends" from work were still coming by to hang out and watch movies. The funny thing was, I was never invited over to join. He would always tell me that it was in my head and that they were only friends. I always knew better. During the time I was pregnant with our oldest daughter, he dropped out of college to work. In the beginning of my pregnancy, he had a great job making about $19 an hour, working with special-needs kids. Things were going great with that job until they lost their funding and he could no longer afford his bills, much less a new baby, but he was trying. He then began working three part-time jobs just to be able to take care of this bundle we had on the way, sometimes not getting enough sleep, but he still did it just to make sure that his new family was taken care of. I can remember times he would leave his warehouse job at 2:30 a.m., come to the apartment, get some sleep, eat breakfast, and catch the bus to the mall to work his other part-time job. He would do his third job on the weekends. I was beyond amazed by Darren's determination and drive. He was proving to himself and me that he could take care of his new family. Darren during that time sacrificed so much to make sure that we were okay—to me, he was my superhero. The one thing that he was during our time together was a great provider. We saved for months to make sure we could buy our daughter the things she needed. We worked together and saved enough so that on a Saturday afternoon we were able to buy her cradle, dresser, and changing table. He went to the store and bought the bedding, clothes, and other baby things she was going to need. We were so proud of what we had done. He had set up her room in his apartment. He decorated the walls with Winnie the Pooh, and all that we needed was our little one.

November 27, 1995, around 7:00 p.m. I was in my mom's kitchen washing dishes and out of the blue I started to feel this pain. It felt like really bad gas so I ignored it. It came and went for a while and I thought nothing of it until it got worse. I went upstairs and tried to wake my mother up but she was sleeping and not fully coherent. I went into the shower to try to ease the pain but nothing was working. My mom jumped out of her sleep when she finally heard what I said and rushed me to the hospital. While en route I called Kim and she went immediately to pick up Darren from his apartment to bring him to the hospital. Before I could make it to labor and delivery Darren was by my side. The pain was getting more intense and Darren kept telling me to breathe and all I wanted to do was kick him in the face. I was squeezing the life out of Kim's hand to the point she thought I broke it. Darren had this look of fear and panic on his face. My dad, who was the only person who kept me calm, walked in and started holding my hand and rubbing my head and said it would be okay and it was. November 28, 1995, at 7:25 a.m., our daughter was born. She was perfect, and I fell in love immediately. Darren stayed with me from the moment I reached the hospital until the day it was time to go home. On that day, I broke his heart. You see, I went back to my parents' house, and he went back to the apartment without the daughter he'd prepared the room for. At the time, I did not realize how badly I had hurt him by doing that. Years later, I sincerely apologized for the moment I could never undo.

After our first daughter was born, life got hard. We were simply trying to make it, but we could barely keep our heads above water. I was living back at home with my parents and he was struggling to keep the lights on in his. To make the situation even more stressful, the constant tension between him and my mom kept me in the middle of two stressful relationships. I was always feeling that I was caught in a battle and never on the winning side. If I sided with one, then the other person would be angry. I was always trying to appease the other person while all along I just wanted everyone to shut up and stop talking. Darren went from being that wonderful young man to "that boy." My mother became so disappointed when I became pregnant that she lashed out at not only me but Darren as well. My mom always thought that he ruined my life and destroyed the dreams that she had for me and he felt that my mom wanted to do the job he was fighting to do and that was raise his daughter. Everything was an argument, whether Darren called and didn't say hello to her on the phone or his tone was disrespectful. He would want to keep our daughter overnight and I would not let him, and that turned into my family was excluding him from his daughter.

There were times that Darren would call and my mom would come in my room and angrily say, "Tanya, tell Darren if he cannot say hello and greet me properly on the phone then do not call my house."

Darren made a major decision after talking to his dad one afternoon. Darren was going to join the military because he so desperately wanted to take care of his new family. We had many conversations about getting married after our daughter was born. Before he left for the service, we had a serious conversation that started with a phrase I'll never forget.

"I heard that single guys shouldn't go to basic by themselves ... "

"Are you saying that if I do not marry you then what?"

"That a lot of things can happen when you get to basic."

"So, again, if I don't marry you then I have to worry about you leaving for someone else?"

"That is not what I am saying. All I said was my pops told me that single guys shouldn't go to basic by themselves."

When he the uttered those words, I knew that if I did not marry this man he would leave me. So in September 1996, at the justice of the peace office, we were married. No one else was in that room but the two of us and the justice. I remember thinking, *I do not want to do this but if I don't he will leave me.* When we walked out of the courthouse I felt no more married than I did when I walked in. There were no rings exchanged but two simple life-altering words ... *I do.*

Advice to my former self, my daughters, and to you, my readers: *Your wedding day, whether it is in front of hundreds or just the justice of the peace, ought to be a day filled with special memories. It should be filled with love and newness. Never be afraid of being alone because sometimes that is exactly where God wants you to be so that he can show you how beautiful your life can be. Do not hold on to anyone out of fear. That is not love, and fear is not of God. To hold on to the wrong person for the wrong reasons is simply cheating yourself out of endless possibilities.*

CHAPTER TWO:
I DO

IN OCTOBER 1996, Darren left for basic training, and that started our military life. He would be gone for 12 weeks. What was I going to do without him? Lord knew I missed him. I looked forward to the phone calls he would sneak in just to say, "Hey, I miss you and the baby so much. I love you guys. Remember I am doing this for you guys."

That was all I needed to get me through the day. In December 1996 I went to his basic training graduation in Columbia, South Carolina with our daughter, and I was so proud. In my mind he looked so handsome in his class A uniform. We left from there and went to his father's home to spend the Christmas holiday together. Darren left to go run some errands and I decided to be helpful to get some of his things out of his suitcase. As I was pulling out some of his clothes I saw a manila envelope marked "letters." Thinking how sweet that he saved my letters I opened up the envelope but what I thought was my penmanship and my letters belonged to another woman. I came across letters from a woman he went to basic training with, and what I read hurt so badly. They talked about our daughter and how she was proud that he was such a good dad but there was no mention of a wife. It talked about them being together and how she was already missing him. Her words sounded just like the same words that I wrote him. My head was spinning and I was becoming angry. I started going through some more of his things to see what else he was hiding.

I could not believe that we were back in this place, a place of lying and cheating. In my mind I just knew that once I was his wife that all the lying and cheating would stop. I wanted to believe anything he said. I held on to the lie as though it were the truth. But my head already knew. How many times do we settle for less in life just to keep someone in our lives? Well, for me, far too many. In January 1997 he left again to go to advanced individual training. We spoke every weekend and I looked forward to his calls. Then one weekend I didn't get my usual call. I kept running upstairs to check my phone, and there was not one missed call. I was nervous because this was not like him. Then that Sunday afternoon, he finally called and told me that he was arrested for hitting this guy who called him a racial slur. I made myself believe it because I just knew that he would not cheat. He loved me way too much. He promised me that he would never hurt me. He knew what I had been through before. Darren was aware of my past relationships where being faithful was never a key element.

Well, a year and a half later, baby number two had arrived. I was 5,000 miles away from my family and friends, living in another country, and he was on his way to another deployment. I decided to call this random number that was all over my phone bill, because something in my head said that something wasn't right. When I had previously asked him about the number he said it was a friend's number, but I knew that he was lying. So when the young woman's mother told me the whole story, I believed it.

Yes, my husband went down to North Carolina the weekend Darren said he was arrested for hitting that guy, and yes her daughter knew he was married, but she loved him. When I ended that phone call the room was spinning and the tears were streaming. I wanted to run away and never come back, but I thought, *Who would want me?* I would be alone, raising two babies by myself.

So I stayed.

It was not easy to stay even after seeing another woman's photo in my husband's duffle bag, seeing that she was special enough to be nicknamed, and running into her inside the post office on the military installation that I lived on. I knew that he was going away for the weekend with another woman but saying that he was leaving for a rugby game (our friends later confirming). Or staying after your husband has another woman plan his promotion party while I was only given an invitation to attend. My pride, my heart, and my self-worth had reached an all-time low. I just kept quiet. I was hurting so much but I still did not walk away.

Advice to my former self, my daughters, and to you, my readers: *Never place a price on your pride, your heart, your self-worth, or your love! You are more valuable than that! Love yourself and when you do, God will send your way the right man that was created just for you. Do not hold on to the wrong one for the wrong reasons. That is not going to make him love you the way you deserve; it simply means that you settled. Life is not about settling; it is about living. Never allow anyone to treat your love like it's commonplace. You are a gift, a divine, hand-crafted gift, and should be treated as such. When you value yourself as common then that is how you will be treated. You are not common. Always remember that you and all that comes with you are divine. I love you, girl. You might not know it, but you will be okay because I will not allow us to fail.*

CHAPTER THREE:
BETRAYED

AFTER LIVING OVERSEAS, we moved back to the States. Texas became our new home, and I thought things would get better. For a while it seemed as though they did. We laughed, we joked, but we also argued. We would argue about everything from how we should discipline the girls to my family calling, or calling too much, as Darren would say.

"Why is your mom calling here so much?"

"She just wants to talk to the kids."

"She doesn't have to call every day. This is my home and it will not be run by your mom."

"First of all, my mother is not running this home, and just because she wants to be involved with her grandchildren, what is wrong with that? It's not like your father cares."

"Just because Pops doesn't call doesn't mean he doesn't care, and the girls could call him too."

"It's not their responsibility to foster the relationship with your dad, it's his, and if he cared enough, he would, but I get it, because your father could care less and my parents care too much."

We could not go two days without a major falling out. It got to the point that our eldest daughter would say, "Please don't fight."

The damage we did to our children can never be undone. The fearful look in my babies' eyes was a clear indication that they knew that their parents were going to break up. Sometimes the fights got so bad I would pack up the girls and leave. Darren would often say that I did not talk to him, but I would talk to my friends. That statement was true. I found it easier to talk to my friends than my own husband. I trusted my friends and could not trust my husband. The years of dishonesty made it to where my heart was turning. But despite how I felt, I stayed. Many times I fought myself to stay. There were so many times I simply wanted to pack up my daughters, the fish and the dog, and leave, but all the while thinking what would my children think about me?

Advice to my former self, my daughters, and to you, my readers: *There are two places in this life you ought to have peace: your house and your grave. Now you have no control over the grave, but you do have control over your house! When you put the key into the door where your name is on the lease and you feel burdened, then there is a problem. When you are dreading going home, then it might be time to start cleaning house.*

We struggled to become financially secure. There were times we did not know how we were going to keep the lights, water, and cable on. We pinched pennies to make sure Christmas and birthday parties for our children were great. We worked together to make their lives as normal as possible. He was the only one working and I was babysitting to help out. When I finally found a full-time job, things got a little better. The pressure was not only on his shoulders: we were trying to get ahead together. We were repairing our credit together and getting our lives back on track. Darren no longer wanted to be in the military and felt that he could work on post making more money. I supported that because I wanted him home. The deployments and field exercises made me feel like a single parent at times. I wanted a normal family—two parents with their children eating dinner together every night. I wanted the life that most women dream about. I wanted to be the family with the husband and wife who were raising their children, going to church, and attending the kids' sporting events together. For about a year, we had that. He was home every night. We had family game night every Thursday and restaurant night every Tuesday. He was the coach for our youngest daughter's soccer team. He was the "soccer dad." I was the "soccer mom," and I loved it. We had some great times. We watched our daughters excel in sports and exceed in school. We built our first "dream home," and we were working together. Not many people can build a custom home from the ground up as their first home. We picked out the carpets, the backsplash, the corner lot, and the brick color. Everything in that house was built by our design. Moving into our first home was exciting, and we thought that we were well prepared, but life got tougher. We were both working, but nothing really prepares you for the financial responsibility of running your own home.

We were definitely not prepared. I knew he always wanted his own business, so we started a cleaning business. For a while it was working. It was bringing in extra income and things were going well. We were running our own business. Then one of our major competitors began getting all the work and we had to close down. It felt like we were back at the beginning. Money quickly became tight; the mortgage payment was getting behind and we struggled to keep afloat. We were so financially pressed that we had to make a decision that changed the course of our marriage forever. God knows I did not want him to go, but we had kids to feed, and a roof to keep over their heads.

So in June 2005, he left to go to Iraq. That was a hard day for me; there were so many worries that went through my mind. But all he kept saying was we have a plan—two years tops and he would be back home. Two years came and went, and Darren never came back for good. When Darren left, our two daughters were in elementary school. I instantaneously became a single parent, but I did not complain because my life had always been about my children. Their happiness was my primary focus. I did everything I could to make sure that even though their dad was not there, they would not miss out on anything.

THE MOMENT I DECIDED TO OWN IT

I still maintained my full-time job so that the money I was making went to the girls. They enjoyed life as they had always known it, with our restaurant night on Tuesdays, the family game night on Thursdays, and we added a pizza night on Fridays. Our weekends were filled with soccer games and church, so we stayed on the go. That kept us busy. The pressures of life were starting to weigh me down. I began to feel like I was doing everything on my own. I was working, taking care the kids, running the house, and making sure the bills were paid. This also included getting the girls back and forth from soccer games and practices and getting them to and from school along with their regular everyday life activities. I felt alone and that I was in this fight by myself. There were days I was just angry, feeling as if he had abandoned me and wanting to scream, but I kept silent. Some days I just wanted to lie in the bed, but I couldn't because I had people who depended on me. I could never allow my daughters to think that giving up and going into seclusion was the answer. I wanted them to know strong women get up every day and handle the business of life. I would often tell my daughters that life does not stop because you are having a bad day, so shake it off and keep it moving. Even when I did not want to I had to continue to set the example. Being weak was not a choice. If I did not expect my daughters to stop living, I had to keep it moving myself.

I started to feel myself drowning, not only because of the pressures of everyday life, but because he was also constantly telling me what I was doing wrong in his absence. There was never a phone call expressing gratitude for all that I was doing on the home front. It was always something that I was not doing right in his eyes. It was either I was not starting a business or was not finding homes for him to buy or saving enough money. I would often say, "What more do you want me to do?"

I will never forget the day that I came across an email that was to one of his ex-girlfriends. In the email he never called me his wife—I was just "her." I was so angry and hurt by his blatant disrespect. After the "I am sorry" and the "She is just a friend," it still did not ease the pain I was feeling. It did not make me feel any better. All I wanted to do was lie in the bed under the covers with the lights off and sleep, but I could not do that because my babies depended on me. Life did not stop, and my children did not stop needing me because of my continual disappointments. I had to put a smile on my face and keep living. But no sooner did I try to get past that, when there was yet another email to a "friend" saying how he missed their showers together.

This time I would handle it differently. I just kept quiet on the outside, but on the inside I was erupting. You see, I just got tired of talking because at that point nothing was going to change. Lord knows I was mad as hell. I was mostly mad at myself because I was afraid to make a necessary change in my life, always thinking if I walk away the other woman would win. This was a game—I was playing Russian roulette with my heart.

THE MOMENT I DECIDED TO OWN IT

Advice to my former self, my daughters, and to you, my readers: *Never stay because you think by leaving the other person is winning. By staying you are the one losing, losing out on a love that is meant for you, losing out on what life, love, and marriage is all about. Always heed the warnings and never be complacent with your life. You control it. Never allow anyone or anything to take that from you. Never be the victim in your own life.*

CHAPTER FOUR:

MARRIED, BUT SINGLE

DARREN'S FIRST OVERSEAS JOB as a government contractor barely kept us afloat. He worked on the fuel line and he would work seven days a week, twelve hours a day. People would often believe because you are working overseas that you were doing well, but with the first contract that was not the case. He was making a little more than his previous stateside job as an aircraft mechanic. We held many conversations over the phone regarding his pay and he felt that he could be back in the States struggling rather than being overseas and away from his family. We agreed that before his contract came to an end Darren would look for a job stateside. As I prepared for his return he called me one evening and told me of an opportunity that he could not pass up.

"Hey, babe, remember McTarlin from Germany?"

"Yeah, I do. How is he doing?"

"He is pretty good. He is over here with me and was telling me about his job and how much he is making and that they are hiring and he will give me a good recommendation."

"I thought we said you were coming home."

"We need to get ahead and coming home will not make us enough money to do that and start my business so that I do not have to work for anybody."

"We really want you to come home. I don't want to raise our children by myself."

"All we need is two more years and then I will be home. We will have enough money saved and I can start flipping houses."

He figured the best thing for us was to start our own "separate" accounts because he felt we could not save with a joint account.

"And with this new contract I think we should have separate accounts so that I can have better control over the money and we can save."

"So now with a better job that's what you want you want to do?"

"Listen, don't argue with me about it. Just trust my plan."

That statement stung, but I did not complain. I fell back and I watched. I gave him a budget plan to implement and for the first four months it was working. Darren was saving and he was following my budget. Then tragedy struck—death. His grandmother died, and his world was rocked. I remembered that day I had to make that call to Darren. It was a late in the evening and the girls were already in bed. I was sitting on the bed in our bedroom, holding my head in my head as I told him.

"Hey, babe."

"Hey, babe. What's going on?"

"Nothing much, but what are you doing right now?"

"Getting ready to get up and start my day. Did you just want to hear my voice?"

"Always, babe, but I need to talk to you about something."

"What's going on?"

"Are you by yourself?"

"Yes. What's going on?"

"Babe, I am so sorry, but your grandmother passed away tonight."

His voice started to quiver and he said, "What? I need to get home."

I could hear the pain and anguish in his voice and all I wanted was to hold him and let him know I was here. Trying to make everything stress-free for Darren, I had everything in place when he stepped off the plane from car rental to hotel reservations. The children and I flew in from Texas to North Carolina to be there and support him. No sooner had we gotten there then all the spending took place: dinners for the entire family of almost $500 a meal for seven days, or going on shopping sprees and all I did was sit back and watch. All the money we had saved was spent. I told him that we could not afford to do things like that. We could not afford to blow money recklessly. Darren turned and looked at me and said, "I work hard and can spend my money when I need to."

A few months later Darren invested thousands in a shell company thinking he could use that to buy houses. We never discussed it, nor did we have a conversation about it—he simply went out and did it. When the paperwork came to the house, I hit the roof and, Lawd, did we argue over that. I told him there are no get-rich-quick businesses. You have to take your time, save, and buy one house at a time. Darren never listened when I tried to tell him that.

When that failed, of course it was my fault. He felt as though I was not supporting his dream. Frankly I will support anything that makes sense, but it never did. Darren was buying expensive watches and colognes that he never wore because he was always gone. Who has over 50 bottles of cologne but only uses one or two of them for a couple of weeks a year? Darren! Who sends over a $1,000 to a "friend," and when the "friend" asks, "Are you sure your wife will not mind"? Darren's reply was, "What does my wife have to do with me helping a friend?" but then turned around and blamed me for not being able to save money.

I remember saying, "Maybe you are FDIC insured, and that is why you can spend and give away money with no thought for tomorrow." We went back to the savings plan, and again it worked, or so I was told. In September 2008, my personal world was rocked. My grandfather whom I loved dearly passed away, and that single moment changed my way of thinking. I loved being out in Texas on my own, having to stand on my own two feet, but when he died I felt alone and away from my family. I made a decision; I wanted us to be closer to both of our families. Life is short and you never know when you are going to lose someone important to you.

"I think we need to move closer to our family."

"WHY? I like Texas."

"So do I but our parents are getting older and when things happen we can't get to them as quickly being here in Texas."

After much discussion we moved to Georgia in June of 2009.

Advice to my former self, my daughters, and to you, my readers: *Never be clueless about your finances. Always be an active participant. Never let someone have complete control over your money. Separate accounts lead to separate lives. You must be able to hold each other accountable. In any relationship there should be no secrets, especially in your marriage.*

We started settling into our new home and preparing for him to go back to work (overseas). Then, one day the bombs starting going off. Bomb number one: I came across something that took me again to the place of mistrust. Darren had a Magic Jack, and it kept a phone log. I came across many late-night phone calls with several different numbers. One was from the woman who planned his promotion party while we lived in Germany. He would tell me he was asleep when he was actually on the phone with her. A liar is a liar and a liar all day. I instantly hit the roof. I went from 0 to 100 in 60 seconds, and, like always, it was my fault because I went through "his" things. You see, when the other person is caught, they will always shift the blame onto you to deflect the blame.

The following day he received an email from his job where they told him that his services with the company were no longer needed. There went bomb number two! And bomb number three? We had no money saved! Who works overseas making excellent money, making more money in three months than teachers make all year, and there is nothing left? All the while people on the outside looking in think that you have it all together. That was the furthest from the truth. I sat back and I took it all in. I did not yell or scream about bomb two or three. I just began to think of a way to make sure we did not lose everything. My birthday was a few days later, and we went out for a family dinner.

While sitting at dinner at this quaint, cozy Cajun restaurant that Darren found we were talking and made the decision to again get our family back on track and work hard doing that. I looked at him wearing his blue jeans and his plain button-down polo shirt during dinner, thinking to myself, *Do I want to put myself through this again and try to put my heart back into this relationship?* I again overlooked my personal feelings about what my gut was telling me and chose to put them aside. While we were discussing our finances (again) he felt that the only way we could get back on our feet was for him to go back overseas. I hated the thought but we really did not have much of a choice. He had some contacts overseas, and one was offering him another overseas job in counterintelligence. Again, the "All we need is two years" conversation came up. I remember saying when I got married I thought it meant I would have a husband whom I would see every day.

CHAPTER FIVE:
NEW ADDITION

AUGUST 2009, AT 3:15 P.M., was a life-changing day. My cousin kept telling me that something was wrong. I smelled everything, and every smell was strong and intense, giving me a headache. I was sleeping all the time and not even realizing it. I would close my eyes for what I thought was a second and the next thing two hours had gone by. At the urging of my cousin, I took a pregnancy test, which I knew would be negative. As I was in the bathroom urinating on the stick before it was complete the test read ... pregnant! Unplanned and so unexpected, I was not thinking I would be starting over. Our daughters at the time were 13 (almost 14) and 12. I said nothing for two days. On an early morning in August I was awake around 3:00 a.m. because I was trying to figure out how I was going to tell him before he got on the plane to go back overseas.

Darren woke and asked, "What's wrong?"

I asked the question that I asked two other times before: "How much do you love me?" and he instantly knew. Now going back overseas was not a choice, it was a need. We had a baby on the way. While I was still pregnant with our first son, he came into contact with an old friend and his wife. They both wanted to purchase real estate and figured that going into partnership together would be the perfect idea. She told him that she had contacts and Darren had the financial resources to make it work. They started talking about going into business together, and he kept me out of the conversations. Darren later told me that he felt I would have had something negative to say. They found a gentleman who could help them purchase large commercial properties, and for only $25,000 he could make Darren's dream a reality. Without talking to me or thinking about the fact that we had a baby on the way he invested the entire $25,000. Guess what. They did not purchase the hotel and the money was gone! I was so angry. I cursed, cried, and cursed some more. He felt that sharing this with me was not important, even though $25,000 was gone, never to come back. I thought he would have learned from losing his job and having nothing to fall back on. I hoped that he would do things differently, but no, he did not. In April 2010, I had to be at the hospital at 5:00 a.m. to be induced. I was starting to retain a lot of fluids, and in two days I gained 10 pounds of retained water. My kidney was no longer working properly, and the doctor said we could wait no longer.

Both my father and sister were there with me that day. I was breathing through the contractions without medication. Then a few hours later the doctor said that my progression was slow, and they decided to break my water. In my mind the floodgates of hell opened up, and the pain was excruciating. I begged for an epidural but I had to wait until I had two bags of IV fluids, which took almost two hours. After 11 hours of labor and 45 minutes of pushing, six pounds and two ounces later the third-greatest blessing was born—my son.

He was perfect. The moment was perfect, and his dad was flying back to meet his son. The next day around 8:26 a.m., Darren met our son, Donavan. As he was holding him, Darren asked me something that changed my heart.

"Are you sure this is my son?"

I was hurt beyond words. I was confused, and all I wanted to do was cry. Again, I simply said, "Yes." I was discharged a couple of days later, and we were taking care of Donavan in shifts. During my shifts I would breast-feed, and during his shifts Darren would bottle-feed. We were still exhausted, but we were working together. A few days later I woke up with a searing headache. I could not move without the pain intensifying. I took all sorts of pain relievers, but nothing worked. When I first told him what was going on, Darren said, "Well, just lay down," without thought or any concerns. I tried to lie down but the pain in my head was so intense I thought I was going to die. I suffer from migraines but nothing to this extent. I had never felt anything of this magnitude, and when I tried to explain it he again said, "Well, just take something for it."

I endured this pain for hours. My sister was there and suggested that I take my blood pressure so I did and my blood pressure read 184/130. I called my doctor, and she instructed me to get to the ER immediately. When my sister and I arrived at the emergency room they took my blood pressure again and this time it read 220/184. I thought I was going to have a stroke. I was in room 3, and all I heard was crying. The patient in room 1 died, the patient in room 2 died, and the patient in room 4 died. Lord knows I thought I was next. They first ran a CAT scan and said they saw a mass in the front in my brain. I had so many thoughts in my mind. *Who will take care of children? My baby boy will never know me.* I was an emotional mess.

They did test number two, a CAT scan with a dye, and then they said it looked like a growth but they would do a MRI the next day. I became even more emotional, thinking, *I am not ready to die. I have to be here with my children.* My sister left, thinking that Darren should be there with me, holding my hands, wiping my tears, and reassuring me that everything was going to be okay. When Darren came all he asked was, "When are they going to let you go home?" because he was tired. Again, I was hurt. There was no concern about my health. No questions about what the doctors told me. No questions about how I was feeling. No words of encouragement, just that he was tired and he had the kids all day. I thought, *You are complaining and you are only here two or three weeks every six months and you are tired after one day. I do it all the time.*

Darren left to go home. I stayed in the hospital by myself and again felt unloved and alone. After several tests they found that I had an entanglement of veins called an AVM, or arteriovenous malformation. That is an abnormal connection between arteries and veins. The pressure of the pushing during the labor caused some bleeding in my brain. Per the doctor's orders I had to reduce my stress level, watch my diet, and come back every six months to make sure that there was no more bleeding. I listened to what they had to say but all the while thought, *They must not know what my household was like.* Rest, no stress, and a balanced diet—that would be nearly impossible for me. I had to keep my blood pressure under control and I was on blood pressure medicine for the first time in my life.

Darren left shortly to go back overseas. I was ready for him to leave. I was feeling as if I no longer wanted him there but I thought, *He is only home every six months for two to three weeks.* I could tolerate him that long. But the feelings of love I used to have were gone. The things Darren said and how he treated me made the callouses on my heart harder.

Advice to my former self, my daughters, and to you, my readers: Never allow anyone to mistreat you! Always remember your love is a gift, a priceless gift. Never let anyone treat you otherwise! Your spouse should be there to hold your hand in your darkest hour, laying aside their personal feelings. When stressful situations arise they should be your anchor. Their love should be demonstrated at your weakest moment. When sickness arises, they should be your advocate.

CHAPTER SIX:
ARE YOU SERIOUS? (TWINS)

I N OCTOBER OF 2010, Darren came home on his scheduled R&R, and my feelings were all over the place because when he was home in April, he asked me something that did something to me that could never be undone. I was not going to allow how I was feeling toward him to spoil this time for him and the kids, but I was quiet. We still took care of things around the house like we always would on his R&R and spent time doing the things the girls enjoyed doing. He came and left. During his time home the one area we never argued was our sex life. That seemed to be the only thing that we maintained and did right. Even at the times when I could not bear to see his face, there was something about him that I could not seem to get away from. The way he would look at me or even touch me could start a moment between Darren and me. He could sweet-talk me like no other and I fell for it every time. I used to always say nighttime was our best time. Nothing eventful happened, or at least that's what I thought.

In January 2011, I went in for a regular yearly checkup. The doctor had me urinate in a cup and had me wait in the waiting room. The nurses called my name and asked me to go to room 290-B. Thinking nothing of it, I went. The doctor came in and asked, "How are you doing?"

"I'm fine."

"Well, you're pregnant."

"The hell I am!"

"Yes, you are."

She asked me to lie back so that she could measure me.

"You're measuring at 16 weeks."

"That is impossible because my husband was not home 16 weeks ago."

"Well, maybe it's because you just had a baby. That is why you are measuring bigger but let's do an ultrasound."

I waited in the waiting room until it was time to go into the exam room and lay on the table for my ultrasound. She turned that machine on, and I looked at it really confused. I saw two circles and I said, "Ma'am, what is that? Because if it is a two-headed freak of nature, I will be headed to the clinic."

She smiled. "Well, there are two heads, but there are four legs, four arms and two bodies."

I was in complete shock! Not only pregnant, but pregnant with twins! I was floored. I cried, cursed, and cried some more. I took a picture of the ultrasound machine and instantly emailed it to him. I came home and cried yet again. In my

THE MOMENT I DECIDED TO OWN IT

mind all I kept thinking was, *Five kids? What is this man going to say to me? My life is a wrap!* When he called me he said, "What was in the email?"

"We are having a baby and not just one."

Later that evening Darren called and said he wanted to talk. I was lying in the bed under my covers with the lights off, still in disbelief and trying to process what the doctor and the ultrasound machine told me. Darren started the conversation.

"What are you doing?"

"Nothing. Lying in the bed trying to figure out if this is a bad joke."

"Do you have twins that run in your in family? Because I called Pops and he said we did but three generations back."

"My mom's side has twins two but like yours three generations back."

"What if I told you I had a vasectomy?"

My response was, "I guess it didn't work."

Guess who never had a vasectomy? Darren. Even though I knew in the back of my head that he never had one it started to make me feel angry. I would often wonder what he was trying to imply. Was he trying to say that these could not be his babies? Or that I was cheating? My pregnancy with the twins was as normal as it could be. I was back and forth with doctor appointments, since I was considered high risk due to the medical issues that arose with my previous pregnancy. They were progressing normally, and my due date was July 2011, but the doctor decided that in June 2011, they would make their grand entrance. Well, the twins had other plans: late one

Monday night in mid-May, around 11:00 p.m., I was lying in bed watching television and on the phone with my sister, telling her something was just not right. I was experiencing pain, pain that in my mind was again gas, but this time it came very intense and painful, and in my mind I knew that I could not be in labor. I got up and started cleaning my house just in case something was happening because I simply refused for anyone to come to my home and it not be clean. I woke up around 5:30 the next morning to get my oldest off to school, and when I went to the bathroom there was blood in my panties. I decided to call my doctor and he asked the regular question, "Did you have intercourse last night?"

"No."

I was instructed to come on in. I asked him if I should go to the office and his reply was, "No, to Labor and Delivery."

Well, I had things to do because I was here by myself, and I needed to make sure that my kids were going to be okay for a few hours. I thought I was coming home that afternoon.

I got up, took a shower, drove my eldest daughter Sarah to the high school, and had Heather, my other daughter, stay home with her brother. I called my cousin to come to the house to help my daughter, and I then called my aunt and grandmother. I waited for them to arrive before I left so I made breakfast for my son and made lunch for when he woke up from his nap just in case I did not make it back in time. When they arrived I made sure everyone was okay and then drove myself to the hospital, contractions and all.

THE MOMENT I DECIDED TO OWN IT

When I arrived I checked in around 9:45 a.m. and the nurse asked if I drove myself. I said, "Yes, ma'am. I did."

They looked at me as if I'd lost my mind. After they did the regular check, the nurse said to me, "Well, you are not going home today."

"Oh, yes, ma'am, I will. I have children at home who need me."

"Well, that will not be happening today and when you do go home you will not be pregnant."

I looked and said, "Ma'am do whatever you have to do but I have to get home and take care of my kids."

I have to pick Sarah up from school, I thought. *Is Donavan okay without me at home?*

Then she politely told me, "You are 5.5 centimeters dilated; you cannot go home."

I started making phone calls. I called my parents and my cousin, who packed up their lives and drove from Florida to Georgia that day to come take care of my kids. The doctor came in and said, "Well, we are going to try to stop your labor."

Nothing was working, so at 5:30 p.m. she came in and said, "Well, we tried but they are coming, so we are going to get you ready for your C-section."

I was scared and thought, *Lord I may not have wanted any more kids, but please let my babies be okay.*

My aunt and my grandmother came up to the hospital, and my aunt went in the operating room with me. As I was lying there my head began to pound, and my vision became really blurry. The doctor said that they were going to move fast to get the twins out because Baby A was distressed. At 7:00 p.m. on a warm spring Tuesday evening in May 2011, eight weeks early, my three-pound two-ounce Tiffany was born, but I could not see, touch, or kiss her. She was not breathing well and not very responsive. Then at 7:02 p.m., Trevor was born, coming in at three pounds nine ounces—I got to see him and kiss his cheek before they took him away. The neonatologist came in after I came out of recovery and was telling me about my babies. I started crying because he said that they would be in the NICU for at least three weeks. The baby girl was having the hardest time. All I wanted to do was hold my Tiffany and Trevor, but I could not even get out of the bed. The nurses brought pictures of the babies and I cried. I made my cousin Sidney go to the NICU to lay her eyes on them. They would not let her in at first and she told them under no circumstance was she coming back to my room without seeing the babies. That she did not know how they were going to do it but she needed to see them. Sidney brought me back pictures per my request. There were tubes coming from everywhere and they were covered up. That was a hard time for me because all I wanted to do was hold them and keep them close.

 I stayed in the hospital for four days and my heart was torn when I had to leave because I had never left the hospital without my babies. As my dad pushed me past the NICU on the day I was discharged I cried some more. My family stayed with me until the following Monday, and then it was back to just the girls and me. Life did not stop, and my kids at home still needed things. I had to load up the truck, drop them off to school, come home and take care of my Donavon, and then do the afternoon pickups. The good thing was that they only had one more week of school. I would check on the babies throughout the day, pump bottles to take to the hospital, and when Sarah and Heather were home I would drive to the hospital to see them. One of the nurses asked me one day, "Mrs. Armstrong, did you drive up here?" I lied and said, "No," and she proceeded to tell me that if I had that they were going to have to admit me because I could cause my stitches to rip or cause internal bleeding. All I could think was, *I have to do what I have to do to take care of all of my kids.* Life did not stop because I had babies. I had to keep moving so that everyone was taken care of. I did this every day until they came home, sometimes three times a day. When both babies came home, I felt overwhelmed but complete. All my babies were under the same roof. I felt relieved. Darren came home three weeks after the twins were released from the hospital, and we fell into the routine of mom and dad, but not husband and wife. There was not a lot of affection between us. I knew that the end was coming. I remember sitting on the front step of our house after an argument, and I looked at him and said, "When are we going to call this?" but like always, we swept it under the rug.

We never really talked about our issues, and he would say, "Let's talk." But it is so difficult to talk to a person you don't even trust. Like always, he left. Life again had settled back into a routine ... married but single parenthood.

Advice to my former self, my daughters, and to you, my readers: *Never let someone, anyone, make you feel like a burden. Never allow someone to steal the joy from your life and suck out all the happiness. Never exchange anything for your happiness, especially because you are afraid of change. Never allow anyone to challenge your integrity and morals because they lack it within themselves. Never let anyone challenge your character when they lack character. Never let anyone change the heart of who you are. Never let anyone make you feel that despite your current situation, you are stuck, because you are never stuck. You are and will always be a fighter. Never let a broken man break you.*

CHAPTER SEVEN:

SINGLE PARENT

SEPTEMBER 2012 WAS A REGULAR DAY, and Darren sent me the information for the online purchase he made for the twins. I looked over the receipt, and something was wrong, extremely wrong. I saw two boxes of pampers, baby wipes, and a box of condoms. I looked twice and then looked again. I picked up the phone and dialed his international number. It rang several times and then he finally answered. I was very calm and I asked, "How many people are you sleeping with beside me?"

"What?"

"How many people are you sleeping with beside me?"

"Why?"

"So you order a box of condoms while you are overseas? Are you practicing safe sex with yourself?"

"A friend of mine saw that I was ordering some things off of Amazon and asked me to get them for him."

"Okay."

When he called back later that night, he had the nerve to ask, "Do you still even care?" "Yes. Why?"

"Because you did not even yell or argue."

"Why? Would it have even changed the answer you gave me?"

You see, in my head I already knew that another grown man is not going to ask another man to buy him condoms. I was thinking in the back of my head that I no longer cared enough to argue.

Advice to my former self, my daughters, and to you, my readers: *When you stop talking about a situation, that means that you have either accepted it or you are done with it. Either way, do not become complacent. Make a decision and whatever you decide to do, plan your response! Never make a decision in the heat of anger; just plan your response.*

Four months later, in December 2012, I did it. I went into his email because his tone with me had been indifferent and cold. I read an email between him and a former mistress, and the funny thing about a liar and cheater is they always a find way to make it your fault. It's never your fault! He lied and denied it and then said it only happened once—bull! I was far from stupid. Then he turned around and blamed me, saying that I should not have gone digging in his email and bringing up something that he had already dealt with in the past. Now I was making him deal with it again, making him relive that experience, and having to experience this "shame" again. I was floored that he was blaming me again! He tried to make me feel as if this was my fault, that I caused this, and I had no right to question him. Again, I was quietly contemplating this conversation. Well, a few weeks later all hell broke loose. Toya (his mistress) forwarded me all of their emails, and I was in complete and total shock. He denied being the father of my children, and she only knew about the girls. She never knew the last three even existed. He told her that we were divorced, and said some really hateful things, but to deny being the father of our children was a blow that I could barely withstand. Who does that? Who says, "Even though they are not my daughters?" He wanted to have a child with her, but questioned me about being the father of our children. The things that he wrote ripped my heart out of my chest. I was beyond hurt. I was mad as hell!

When I got a hold of him, I unleashed a barrage of hateful, mean-spirited nasty words, and I meant every one of them. I told him, "While you are on the outside looking in, there will be someone who will love me and these kids the way you could not. While he is loving me and raising these kids, they will call him Daddy and you Mister and you will be footing the bill for him to do so."

She even went as far to let me know about his current girlfriend and the handful of women he had been with previously. Emails between him and the other woman:

From: Toya***********@gmail.com>
To: Darren<*************@yahoo.com>
Subject: my thoughts

Dear Darren, Well I have spent time now exhaling the thoughts of you and me. Now sit back and really think of what you have done. I don't feel as if you understand where I am coming from. The minute you told me you had kids and a wife, I accepted the fact that you were telling me the truth. But really once you said the kids was not yours, I figure the divorce was going to be over. I notice weeks went by and you haven't told me anything as to why she didn't sign the papers yet. And also why I never saw the proof of you actually having the papers to begin with. You told me you're going to be going home and I asked if you were going to stay in the same house, you told me yeah. Hmm! That didn't settled right with me for real. And I let you be since you said your kids are there. But once you told me the kids' ages I was shocked as to why you had to even be in the house with her. You never assured me while you was home as much as you do here. Days went by and I never got a response from my emails. I never was called. You were too short in your replies. I asked what is going on with her, and you tell me y'all barely talked. Really? You're going through a divorce or a break? I don't understand why she hasn't sign the papers, or why you can't talk to me about her without getting upset. Why would I trust in your words when I need action? I told Diane about you and everything to assure you of my feelings for you. Guess what ... she still wants me through it all. And I can't go back to her since I have given you something that she once had. I am going to take time for myself. I meant the shit I have done for you and with you. It has been years since I even tried to let a man enter my world. I am taking advice from within my soul. I rather remember you as a lesson learned. You can't say of all the things you have done for me, Darren that means it wasn't from your heart. I warned you about my life in how serious I take my life. You know I told you prior to my leave that I need to handle my family and other shit for myself. And at the moment talking to you was not on my list. Through everything though I really f@#&ed myself by falling for you in being left to deal with my emotions. Just to hear the word come out your mouth as to you didn't tell her about me. Darren I shared some sh@# with you that no one knows about me and this situation with you is the primary reason as to why I can't see myself with a man period. I told you before you went home that Diane knows about you and she really think it was a woman all the nights I was leaving her and making love to you. I gave you a lot of me whether you notice it. Sh** just to think about how I would pull the condoms off so you could feel my love for you ... hmm! Boy what a door I had open for you ... I was going through some crazy sh** with Diane prior to you and I ever making love. I told you I never had an affair on her and when I did, I went and told her. Now when we talked before you said you wanted to meet her in sh**. Well now she knows who you are and what you look like and she knows my heart was for you. I told her how you and I was f******* playing house and everything. I feel like I caught myself prior to falling madly in love with you. Glad I didn't get pregnant, at least you would have known I could be honest to allow you to know the truth about that. I promised you before you left when we last made love I told you with every bit of strength in me that I wasn't going to let no one get what was yours. Now you come back acting as if you got to hide what you been doing for months with me. You must not know a woman should feel high about herself. No woman should feel as if her man has made her feel little at all. I wish I didn't go there with you sh**. I can never get back what I gave you Darren. If you want everything you ever bought me back then hey say when and where to meet you. I do not have your house keys anymore. They got thrown out the window ... I told Diane you said I have the better hand in this whole situation since she is still on the hook with me. She took ur keys in threw them out. And told me I was a f****** fool for messing with u in the first place. And she told me I should have known by you not telling ur wife about me, that it was a sign. Darren you told me ur marriage failed and now me and you. Well apparently it didn't cuz she still with u. Since the kids aint yours there no way you would even have to pay child support. I feel you are using the kids to hold on to her. Or maybe she doing that to you. But however it is ... please excuse me out the equation. And for the record please don't ask no friends of mine nothing about me. This issue was between me and u. This is all I have to say.

And then his reply:

From: Darren*****@yahoo.com>**
To: Toya<**********@gmail.com>
Subject: Re: my thoughts

Toya, I have not lied to you about anything. From the time you and I started having feelings for each other I treated you as if your last name was mine. Putting you ahead of all things. I have real feelings for you and I don't regret any of them. You were a breath of fresh air for me, someone I've been wanting to meet but haven't. I did not like talking about my divorce because it upset me a lot. I felt as though I'm a good guy and was a good husband but I got sh*%##ed on and I didn't want to bring that into what you and I were creating. Even though my girls are not my girls, I will still be their Dad and love them to death. And majority of my leave was with them assuring them that Dad will always be there for them regardless of what happens. My world was very small and guarded until I meet you, and let you in. I also shared with you. things that no one else knows or will know. Nobody has seen me in the light that you have. I don't feel like a fool for falling for you and you shouldn't either. I followed my heart even though I knew I could not have you completely. I'm sorry that I didn't assure you that you were in my world and that I was coming back to you. But I never shut down on you as you did to me leaving me to guess as to what was going on with you, us, or what was on your mind. I wasn't given a chance. You just shut me out of your world and told me not to bother you. My whole flight back I thought about us but when I returned that was not the case. I can't read minds and have always said that communication is key but that was not done either. Everything I did for you was from the heart or else I would not have done it. What I did for you I have not ever done for anyone else, that's how I felt for you. The problem between us has nothing to do with me being a man, it has everything to do with you not talking to me, if you would have used a lil of the effort you used in this email to just say to me "hey this is what's on my mind," then we could have went from there. You just said f*** it and f*** me as well. Leaving me feeling confused and hurt. I didn't hear from you while you were on leave, I knew there was a lot for you to deal with at home. I wanted to be there for you but you told me to leave you alone. You cut my legs off and then blame me for not being there. When I was here the entire time just waiting for you to tell me something anything. My first thoughts were that you're pregnant and didn't know what to do. My thoughts were that if you are this will be one loved child and well taken care of, if it's a boy or girl, names, the whole nine. I told my family about you and that this is what I think to be true. I don't regret making love to you unprotected, it was an act of trust and how I felt and I haven't had these kind of feelings for anyone for a long time. To let you know that regardless what happens I'm here. And I would do it all again because I followed my heart instead of guarding it as I have done. It does not surprise me that Diane wants you still. As I said before you two have history, I was the odd man out with my heart on the line. You were going to be ok either way. You're making me out to be the bad guy in this as though I have done you some great injustice and all I have done was want to love you and be that man you have never been with, be there for your every need and then some. And I didn't hide how I felt about you at all from anyone. You became the center

> of my world. I swear I don't know where it went wrong. I treated you as a man should treat a woman, if in any way I made you feel small my apologies. I don't know how that was. I didn't feel I had your heart although that's what I wanted, I felt you were holding back but now that's neither here nor there since you're done with me. Again I don't regret it at all, I thought things would end up differently once we talked. I feel as if good men finish last. I don't have any bad feelings towards you and wish you the best, you will be missed and our times together will be remembered. I'm here if you ever need me. Te' Amo sol.

Can you understand why I became so enraged? He actually wrote these words. I thought to myself, *What kind of man denies his children?* I get that he lied about the wife, but to lie about your children ...

CHAPTER EIGHT:

HE'S BACK!

During the weeks of February and until he came home in March most of our conversations were short or strained. Either we spoke briefly or we simply argued.

I remember a conversation where he stated that since he was paying the bills he was no longer going to send the $500 biweekly to help with the kids and the most he would send would be $250.

"If I am paying the bills at the house you do not need more than $250 every two weeks to take care of you and the kids."

"You realize that groceries need to be purchased, gas in the truck, speech therapy and occupational therapy for Donavon."

"You better figure out a way to make that work."

His reason was the possibility of losing his contract. He was going to need to save and we were going to have to cut back on everything. I simply listened and took a mental note. You see, his conversations with me were changing; there was no more I love you after we ended a phone call. Now he was only calling about bills and if the bills seemed too high then he was calling to argue. He was no longer calling to see how Donavon was doing with his speech or even the twins. The calls to Sarah and Heather seemed less and less. I kept wondering in the back of my mind how this R&R was going to happen if we could not handle simple conversations on the phone.

On March 10, 2013, he was coming home for his three-week R&R. My mind was truly everywhere. I kept wondering how the trip was going to go. My stress level was through the roof and I was bracing myself for whatever came my way. His flight was due to come in around eight thirty that evening. I got dressed in my yellow Gap sweater and dark blue skinny jeans, wearing my canvas sneakers. I left the house around eight fifteen and headed to Hartsfield-Jackson airport in Atlanta. I waited and waited for him to come through immigration. After waiting at the airport I finally saw him around midnight. I did not get excited—no butterflies, no joy, no smile. Just a simple "Hey. How was your flight?"

"It was fine but long. Give me a hug."

We barely hugged each other. He talked as if nothing was wrong and that this was a regular R&R but it was far from it. When we arrived home from the airport he took his bags upstairs to the bedroom and said he was going to take a shower. I changed my clothes and got into the bed. After his shower Darren got into bed and said, "Come lay over beside me."

"Are you sure?"

"Come on."

That is what I did and even though everything within me was screaming not to let him touch me I so desperately needed to be held even by Darren that I scooted to his side of the bed.

As I was falling asleep Darren whispered in my ear, "I've missed you" and then he started to kiss my neck and while my mind was telling me "Tanya don't do it" my body still wanted him. But it was different. There was no connection, no true intimacy, no passion. It was as if we were two strangers. I felt as if I could have been anyone in that bed with him and felt dirty. I went back to my side of the bed and just went to sleep. The following morning after we got out of bed he was headed out to the store to pick up some items he said he was going to take back, and as he was walking out of the door I said, "Something is different, real different," and he said, "Let's just enjoy this trip."

But my gut told me something was wrong, extremely wrong. When he came back from the store with bags and bags of snacks, I asked him what was going on. Again, without hesitation he lied and said that he was bringing the snacks back for him and a couple of the guys who sent him back with their lists, but I sensed he was lying. I did at the time what I needed to do because he simply was not going to be honest, and I went through his international cell phone. What I read inflamed such anger within me. Not even 12 hours after landing back in the States to spend time with his family, and shortly after leaving my bed, he was texting his new mistress, Alexis, and buying her things at the store to take back. All the snacks ($210 worth) that he said were for the guys was a lie. It was all for Alexis because she was living in his room overseas. I came downstairs, threw his phone across the kitchen, and asked, "So this is what we are doing?"

He got up off the sofa and headed in my direction demanding his phone back. I said, "Hell no!"

He proceeded to struggle with me in the kitchen to get his phone, and I threw it again, against the wall. "Look what you did."

"Who is Alexis? Who is this woman?"

"She is a friend."

"Oh, I see. We call all of our friends 'babe.'"

"It's just a term. It does not mean anything."

"What do you want to do, Darren?"

"Nothing is going to change because I am never here."

"Because you already have someone."

"I don't have anyone."

"Stop lying, just stop lying, and for once in your damn life tell the truth."

"I don't want to be in a relationship with anyone right now because I need to focus on myself."

I just sat on the sofa, looked at him, and said nothing. The saddest part of this entire ordeal was it was Heather's 15th birthday, and Darren bought her nothing. If he could make sure that his mistress/side chick/woman or whatever he wanted to call her was taken care of, his children's wants should all be fulfilled. A few days passed, and we were leaving for our final family trip to Jamaica for my cousin's wedding. In my mind all I wanted was for the children to have at least one good memory of their parents together. Darren and I owed them that much because we were about to pull the rug from under them. We had to travel from Atlanta to Orlando to catch our flight. As we were driving in the car, his mistress and I were emailing back and forth. She sent one email that hurt me beyond words.

From: ALEXIS OLIVA
To: Me by Email.

Ok, again I say for the last time ... You really have me confused with the owner of the email address vs. the owner of the phone (text msgs) ... And if you want my husband's information I would be glad to give it to you, because you seriously have me and somebody else mixed up. On another note to YOU, an insecure WIFE ... I take it you and your DEAR husband must be having some problems or some trust issues. So let me school you on this WOMAN ... IF you were playing your role as a WIFE, then your DEAR husband would not be having another woman sending him text messages. And if you are SO secure with your marriage and YOURSELF, then you wouldn't have to be snooping through your DEAR husband's phone or hacking into his emails. SO since you think you have all the sense in the world, don't try to challenge me and tell me I need to get my life right. Cause by the looks of things, evidently you and your DEAR husband ain't got the marriage life right. Get it together booboo cause whomever number that is texting him is definitely not mine. I own a military issued Blackberry and it is not used to be sending text messages to another foolish woman's so-called husband. And by the way, I know many men and soldiers by the name of Dominic, so you also might want to be a little more specific ... but on the real, it really doesn't make me any difference. Because I'm only concerned with MY DEAR husband, Mr. Olivia, and my LEAST concern is wondering about who is in OUR bed with him at night, keeping him warm, or missing him ... cause it will only be ME! So I wish the best for you and you

> DEAR husband DARREN, but being a grown woman with some relationship knowledge ... it doesn't look too good to me from the emails you are sending. No trust???????? The marriage is already dead! And if he is keeping another woman warm at night, then YOU have the problem, not HER (whoever she is). YOU are probably the reason WHY he IS keeping another woman warm at night, LOL LOL LOL ... I really hate to sound so harsh, but I am just tired of these tired ass women who try to go after the female, like it's their fault, when their problem is at HOME. So please, do not email me with anymore nonsense. Put all that energy into fixing your marriage, if there is still hope for it, and enjoy your DEAR husband while he is with you temporarily V/R MRS. ALEXIS OLIVIA

I became quiet, and he asked me what was wrong. I gave him the email to read, and he said, "I don't see where she said anything harsh."

"I am not surprised."

"Can we go on this trip as friends?"

"What does that mean?"

"Do you want to get your freak on in Jamaica?"

"Have you lost your damn mind?"

"Was that too soon?"

All I could do was shake my head. We barely spoke to each other the rest of the car ride. After we arrived in Jamaica, my only request was, since this would be our last vacation as a family, could he let this time be about our family? He could not do that. He made sure to buy her gifts and send her text messages because he did not want her to feel like what she was the "other woman."

He was text-messaging his mistress my feelings that I expressed to him, and again, I as his wife and mother of his children, held no sacred place. After 19 years of being in a relationship, Darren no longer valued my feelings. There was no regard for my heart.

After we returned from Jamaica, the fighting got worse. The day we landed from our trip my mind was somewhere else and his tone was harsh. I remember stopping at the gas station to fill back up for our return trip home and he asked me if I wanted anything. I said no because I was not hungry. In front of all the kids he looked at me at me and said, "Stop being stupid and eat something."

I looked at him with such disbelief. Never in 19 years had he ever spoken to me that way. Tears filled my eyes and my daughters asked was I okay and I simply responded, "I'm fine."

Sarah said, "I wish he would just leave."

I told her, "It's okay. He is just tired from the trip."

CHAPTER NINE:

DNR (DO NOT RESUSCITATE)

AFTER WE ARRIVED BACK HOME, I had to get back to work and he and I proceeded to text-message each other while he was at the local hardware store. He was asking me about some things that were needed at the house. While walking through the store, he stated that he wanted a divorce. I sat at work in complete disbelief that this is how he came to the decision to end our marriage. Impersonal, through a text message, while walking in the store buying toilet paper. I sat there at my desk stunned, thinking he had this planned the ENTIRE TIME. This was his entire plan but I said nothing but "okay."

In his mind that was okay and we could do it all ourselves without attorneys and be finished in 45 days. I thought, *If he thinks that he is going to discard me within 45 days, he has the wrong one.* I immediately started making phone calls to different divorce attorneys until I found the one I believed would fight for me. I never said a word about what I was doing, and all the time he kept saying we needed to talk about how we were going to separate everything. All he kept saying was I could have the truck, the car, the house, and all the furnishings. All he wanted was his clothes and the Mercedes. While he was home he still wanted to do things such as hang out and go to the movies together as if life was normal, but it was far from that in my mind. Darren would say things such as, "See how well we can get along as friends?"

And I was looking at him as if he had completely lost his mind. I said nothing because the entire time I was thinking, *Wait until the day you get on the plane.* You see, at that point I was operating out of anger, hurt, pain, and a lot of disappointment. One day he was straightening up the house, and Darren texted Alexis, "I am tired of straightening up this raggedy-ass house."

She replied, "If she has nothing else to do, why can't she keep the house clean? She is pathetic."

The lack of respect for not just the mother of his children but his wife! I still held that position and for him it meant nothing. A week before he was due to leave, I went into the closet to get my clothes out for work. I saw his pants that he had on the day before sitting on the floor, and I went through his pockets. I found his international blackberry (he started hiding it so he could text Alexis when I was not around), and I went through his messages to her.

The things Darren was saying about me stung, but like all the other times I said nothing. I took the phone and put it in my purse so that I could forward the messages to my attorney.

As I was proceeding to leave the house, he ran outside in his shorts and socks to question me about the phone. I guess something told him to check his pants because he forgot to put the phone in his hiding place. I told him I did not have it, and he threw his hands up in the air and said, "Forget it."

As I was driving to work Darren sent me a text message that read, "I will be out by this afternoon."

I replied, "Okay."

When I got home, guess who had not packed a single bag. You guessed right! Darren had not packed anything. For the remainder of his trip, all I heard about was the phone and how he was going to need the phone or he could lose his job. I remained silent. I will never forget, Donavon had a severe speech delay to the point I thought he might have autism, for which he is still undergoing the evaluation. I had him in everything to get him help. I called home to see how his speech therapy went that Tuesday, and I got no answer. Next, I texted and the reply I received was, "He did okay." When I later found out that Darren shared in detail my son's session information with his mistress, I was livid. Neither one of them was going to a specialist, talking to the audiologist, or dealing with the severe outbursts. How did he think she had a right to know? Her response was, "I cannot wait to meet my new family."

Where do things like this happen? In my dysfunctional home, that's where. One day Trevor was having a temper tantrum, and Darren looked at me and said, "You need to get that under control because if not, you will have a problem on your hands."

All I could do was stare in disbelief and say, "God, life has to be better than this."

The icing on the cake was when I got a phone call from my Sarah and she asked me, "Mommy, who is Alexis?"

I responded, "Who?" and she repeated the question.

I asked, "Why?" and she said, "Because she sent me a friend request on Facebook."

I was in disbelief. There was no way that his mistress reached out to Sarah. I thought that every side chick knew the rules to the game. It became very obvious that the side chick was the main chick. I was now the other woman. I told him that his girlfriend sent our daughter a friend request and even showed him the request. When Darren said something to Alexis, she denied it. He took her word over not only mine but Sarah's. I became beyond angry. All I saw was red: I had to leave the house, and that is what I did. I went to a coworker's that night for about four hours to calm down. For me that was a "Hell no!" moment. Hell no! I don't want my daughters to think this is how you are supposed to be treated. Hell no! I do not want my daughters to think this is how love is supposed to feel: hell no! I do not want my daughters to think this is what married life is about. Hell no! I do not want my daughters to think that they have to settle on a half a man rather than a whole one. Hell yes! I want my daughters to know that their mother valued herself enough to walk away! I wanted my sons to know that real men love their wives and children. That real men are faithful and honor their vows. That real men guard their families with their lives. That real men honor God and their wives. That real men love only one woman. That real men pray for, with, and over their families. During the months before our first court date, he paid the household bills like he promised he would do. A few months after he went back Darren emailed me saying it was unfair that he had to pay bills in a house he does not reside in and that I should take care of them. He proceeded to turn the water and the gas off because those two bills were in his name. Again, going against what the courts had ordered. I remembered thinking, *If I had done what he wanted to do I would have screwed myself.* You see, at first he wanted us to come up with our own agreement. He said, "Well, I will always make sure you and the kids are taken care of." (Lie number 2,345,567!) He knew with me just going back to work that I was not making enough to sustain the bills and the kids. He said he could send me one entire check a month. With that I would take care of everything, or he would pay the three major bills. There were the two mortgages, one home in Texas and the other in Georgia, and the suburban. He would take care of his car payment.

When he left for Afghanistan, that story quickly changed because now he had a new voice in his ear, Alexis. He now felt that he was doing too much. In September 2013 we had our first court date. It was a temporary hearing to get some things in place. When I got up that cool fall morning I was emotional because in my mind it was the beginning of the end. I said, "Okay, Lord, it's you and me today." I got out of the bed and took my shower. My emotions were all over the place. I stood in my closet trying to figure out what to wear and nothing seemed right but I decided to put on black slacks with a green blouse with my black sweater. As I walked downstairs into the kitchen my dad saw the look of concern and worry on my face and, like the wonderful dad he is, prayed with me. As I pulled up to the white three-story building my nerves were starting to get the best of me. I did not know how I would feel seeing him for the first time since I filed the papers. My heart was in my throat and the palms of my hands were starting to sweat. When I got there I was so nervous and not quite sure what to expect. Then I saw him wearing his khaki pants and oversized shirt with an attitude of disgust written all over his face along with his attorney. When I looked at him, I felt nothing, absolutely nothing. It was if we were two strangers on the street. We said not a word to each other. While we were sitting there for hours going back and forth trying to negotiate, he was unwilling to budge on anything. Darren felt it was unfair to continue to pay my dad for childcare or for taking care of the twins and our son, who was undergoing speech, behavioral, and occupational therapy. My dad took him to all these appointments. I could no longer do it since I was now back at work full time. Darren felt that it was unfair for him to pay the mortgage on the house he did not reside in, but the icing on the cake was when he said that he wanted a paternity test on not one, not two, but all five of our children. I was hurt that not only did he do all of what he did, but now he wanted to assassinate my character. When his attorney asked, "Do you object to paying the temporary child support order at this time?" Darren replied, "Not until I get back the results from the paternity test." When he told this to the judge, the judge then became irate and said to Darren, "I have been in here with you people all day and now you want to bring this before you. Just understand that requesting this will light a match within her you may not be able to extinguish so be careful what you ask for but I will order a paternity if you like but I will also remand you to the state until you get this test done." According to him he changed his mind because he had to get on a flight back to Afghanistan that weekend and could not stay any longer than the weekend. The judge ordered that he pay the court-ordered child support and the mortgage on the home, maintain health insurance for the children, and pay the childcare expenses.

Well, after that court hearing, I said to myself, *Okay, we can handle this.*

That Saturday, Sarah had a soccer game, and so early that cool morning I had to meet him to give him back his car. Heather rode with me in the truck, and my dad drove Darren's car. When we got to the meeting spot I said nothing. He saw Heather for the first time in months and the first thing he said to her was, "Whoa, what did you do to your hair?"

After a brief exchange of words and a hug, Darren then came around the truck to see if I brought the other kids, but I did not. You see, Sarah, Heather, Donavon, Tiffany, and Trevor are worth more than a 30-second visit, and they deserve more than that. Well, later on that day Darren came to the soccer game. When he got there he spoke to the kids with little interaction with the younger three. He gave my children 45 minutes of his time and told them he was heading back to Afghanistan and he had to go. How very far from the truth that was. He went to his new home to set up house. Not one time in those three weeks he was in the States did he call or come back to see his kids. What he did do was put $100 in Sarah's hands and left. Not only did he lie to the judge, but he also was still lying to his daughter. Then I get an email from him asking why I was delaying the paternity test. I was confused because I thought that the paternity test issue was over with.

From: Darren<***********@yahoo.com>
To: Tanya<************@yahoo.com>
Sent: Wednesday, December 18, 2013 9:10 AM
Subject: Re: Child Support Payment

The balance due for the paternity testing for ALL 5 children has been paid. In addition to that, I spoke with the representative and according to their notes you DID NOT call to schedule the appointments, I was informed that you only called to check to see if there was a balance due. So, now there is no reason for you to delay this any longer, please call and have the appointments scheduled. And just so that you are aware, I will continue to track this process until I have received confirmation that ALL 5 of the children have been tested. I greatly appreciate your cooperation with this matter.

Lo and behold when he was still stateside, he paid for a paternity test. I just shook my head, but red flags were popping up everywhere. Who took the test if he was supposedly overseas? Well to make a long story short, I had to take all five of my children to the paternity doctor and watch them stand there in a group with a white piece of paper with their ID number.

At that moment, my children were reduced to a number. I was pissed! However, while I was there I laughed and joked with my girls, but on the inside it was killing me to see each one of them get swabbed seven times on each cheek. I wanted to scream, but I could not.

A few days after Christmas he received the information that he needed; in the words of a talk show I watch, in the case of these five children, you are the father. I remember saying, "It's a funny thing what happens when you sleep with your wife: yeah, she gets pregnant with your kids."

Advice to my former self, my daughters, and to you, my readers: *Sometimes we must make really hard decisions and take certain relationships and people off of life support. We oftentimes find ourselves hoping and praying that it will get better and we see no sign of change. We must be strong enough within ourselves to let toxic relationships go! We hold on to things and people because we are afraid. But holding on only keeps you in a place of hurt, anger, sadness, and disappointment. When we pull the plug on the relationships that are unhealthy in our lives we begin to truly heal. I have to learn to put the DNR notice on anything that endangered my happiness and peace of mind. If the relationship is becoming toxic and you tried everything in your power to restore it, slap a DNR on it and LET IT GO!!! Stop using extreme measures to keep a dead situation alive. Stop resuscitating bad relationships and free yourself to find what is truly out there waiting just for you.*

CHAPTER TEN:
HO HO HO, DADDY NO MO

THAT CHRISTMAS WAS GOING to be different because it was all on me this year and I knew that I was not going to be able to give all the big gifts that I had usually done. I tried my best to get them a few big things and some smaller ones while still keeping up the yearly tradition of new pajamas. On Christmas Eve, there was a knock on my door and someone had delivered a box to the house. When I saw who it was from I was confused—it was from Toys for Tots. I remember thinking I did not sign them up for this because even though they may not have had tons and tons of gifts, they still had a lot. I did not think much about it so I put the box up and continued with my Christmas plans.

I had a good friend who was also separated from her husband here with her kids and other family members. We ate, laughed, and opened a few gifts, and the girls did their best to not allow me to feel too bad, but as a parent I did because this was not the Christmas they were used to. Later on that morning Darren called their cell phones and after a brief conversation, I was told Darren was the person who signed Donavon, Tiffany, and Trevor up for Toys for Tots! I was enraged. I could not believe that he signed his own children up for charity. Now please do not misunderstand me, Toys for Tots is a wonderful organization, and I know that they do a wonderful service for families who cannot provide Christmas for their children, but my children were not underprivileged. Their father was making great money each month and could have afforded to buy them gifts, but instead he decided to steal from children who without this organization would not have gotten anything.

I did not say a word.

January was the last child support payment I received, the last time he paid the mortgage, and the last time he paid for childcare. I did not argue with him. I sent him an email regarding the lack of payment for February and again in March. No reply. I continued to work and take care of my children. I could not afford to allow the divorce to make me lose focus from what was most important, and that was my children. Sarah was preparing for her high school graduation and Heather was still heavily involved with her high school athletic career. Donavon was making leaps and bound with his speech delay and was making leaps and bounds with his progress. The twins Tiffany and Trevor were simply enjoying being my rambunctious duo. Even in the midst of my storm I still had silver linings that reminded that everything was going to be okay. One warm

THE MOMENT I DECIDED TO OWN IT

Wednesday afternoon in March 2014, Sarah was on her way home from school and I had something to tell her. Earlier that day I received the email confirmation that her hard work in school paid off. She got accepted into not one, not two, not three, but all four colleges she applied to. Sarah walked into the front door wearing her gray flower dress, hair in a bun, with her book bag on her back, and I was standing at the top of the stairs waiting for to her to come home so I could tell her the great news.

"Do you remember when I told you that hard work pays off?"

"Yes, ma'am."

"Remember when I told that you sometimes in life you will have disappointments even when you work hard?"

"Yes, ma'am. What happened?"

"Well, today is one of those days where hard work pays off because you got accepted into ... " and before I could finish she jumped up three stairs and into my arms. I immediately burst into tears. Even in the struggle I could still find the joy.

April 2014 was our final divorce hearing. I had been at court since 8:45 a.m., and I knew my attorney was going to be late. It made for a long day. I sat in the courtroom and patiently waited. The judge (not my assigned one, but let me tell you God will put the right one on the bench) asked how I was doing and we made small talk while waiting. He handled all the other cases before mine and I was the last one on his docket. He broke for lunch and we resumed at 1:00 p.m. My attorney arrived and I prayed. They did the pretrial in the judge's chambers and I was back to the waiting game. My attorney would text me to email him some documents that he needed that I had. Remember, Darren told his attorney that he lost his job from January to March, that with his new contract he was losing money, and that is why he stopped paying anything. Well, I believe that I am smarter than the average bear, and I found pay stubs for every pay period from January to April. My attorney came out, asked me a couple of questions, and went back to pretrial. At 4:15 p.m., his attorney came out and said to me, "You have a hardworking attorney who fought hard for you."

Then my attorney said, "We have reached a settlement. Come back in the courtroom."

I went back in and listened to what they said. Tears filled my eyes because I received things I did not even ask for. For that I say only by God's grace! I realized that during all of that time when it was looking like it was going his way, God was having me go through all of that to bring me to that moment in that courtroom. When I first walked out the courtroom I was starting to become overwhelmed with emotions. I was grateful that this moment of my life was over. The divorce was over and I could finally breathe. As I walked out of the courtroom the first person I called was my mom and told her everything the judge said and all she kept saying was "Thank you God. Thank you for keeping Tanya and thank you for allowing her to see you restore her even when people tried to work against her." Then I called my girlfriend in Texas who kept me from jumping off the ledge many times when I thought I could not handle any more, and as soon as I started to tell her what happened she started to cry and with tears of joy she started thanking God in the middle of my conversation.

Then later in April, we had a nasty email exchange. I was tired of holding my tongue and letting him say what he wanted. I was tired of always taking the higher road. I was tired of doing what people said and just say nothing. Hell no! I am human, and I went for the throat. I did not care how he felt. I got tired of being tired. Everyone has a right to feel that way. There is no manual on how to act while dealing with a divorce, and some days are better than others.

Email exchange, April 2014:
Email to me from Darren:

Okay, I can understand her being upset about the DNA, and I can and will explain and apologize to her later. However, please let's not make this seem as if you were a "Saint" in this entire marriage, because you were not. We both had our flaws and you know it, that's the ONLY reason I considered having a DNA test done on the Donavon, Tiffany and Trevor. You and your Attorneys self-consciousness caused girls to be tested, so do not throw that one on me. Because if it wasn't an issue on your part, why did you fight so hard NOT to have them tested? That just further let me know that you yourself weren't sure and/or had something to hide. Because you're right, I paid for it, not you. And you are one to question my ability to take care of my responsibilities, I never knew in a trillion years that I would have ever considered marrying a Greedy, Money-Sucking Leech. After all these years of marriage I have ALWAYS taken care of YOU and the kids, and even your "free-loading" "scamming" family. I have worked hard to make sure we had a roof over our heads, cars to drive, money to spend at YOUR leisure, and to afford the luxuries of you splurging and taking trips and flights to wherever (bet you thought I didn't know), I paid for and provided a Nanny for years when you could have taken care of and watched our own kids because to my knowledge you did not have a job, (Oh you must think you are a Real-Housewife of Lawrenceville, huh?). Also, how cruel of you to bank money from the Texas property and have me struggle to make the payments, yes I said struggle, because back during the summer of 2013 I had to catch up on the payments, remember? So, where did all that money go? You're not fooling anyone but yourself Tanya, you have money stashed somewhere. Out of all the years I sent $500 every pay period to your account for your allowance on top of the monies you received from the Rental property with me still paying all the bills ... you do the calculation. And another thing, to have me pay another family member, living rent free, to help take care of his own grandchildren and receive SSI on top of that and I not know about it WOW, you and your people are something else. Tanya I have no sympathy for YOU, the kids YES, you NO. Because now they have to pay for our mistakes and your selfless thinking. I tried to talk this out with you and be reasonable about it all on my last R&R in 2013, but you felt you needed more and acted out of anger and had me served anonymously the day before I left knowing that for (1) I had to fly back to Afghanistan with only 30 days left to respond, and (2) I had no money, only $7 to my name. So you tell me Tanya, the oh so gracious Accountant, how does a husband that makes over $100k a year for the past 8 years have nothing to show for except debt? What was he doing wrong, no as a matter of fact, what was the so-called wife doing wrong? Why would she allow him to be away from his family for so many years ... Oh let me guess, It was all about the money! Yeah, remember you told someone that back in 2013 via text message??? So you shouldn't be upset about anything, because you only stayed in this marriage for financial security, as long as the money was rolling in you were ok, you never considered any options I had to make business propositions so that I could supplement my income and be home with my family. I needed your help years ago so that I could be home with my kids but you chose your single Fab life over your marriage and enjoyed keeping me away. We should have had thousands in the bank, but your carelessness as well got us to this point. So don't keep pointing the finger at me. Also, to calm down any fussies you may have about Alexis Olivia, for the record, she is NOT my fiancée. She is a friend who helped me during a hardship. Yes she let me borrow money to get a lawyer, because she felt sorry for me and felt that it was sickening for a "proclaimed" wife to be so low to spend all my money and leave me without a dime; as if I didn't take care of my obligations while we were married. Also, Alexis has a career and her own money and she does not need me to do anything for her nor do I have to pay her bills. And again, not that it's any of your business, I am storing my belongings at one of her properties and that is where they will remain until I find me a place to live upon the end of my contract. Please keep her name out of this situation, because if it was such a big issue why didn't you just put her name in the divorce filings??? ... Exactly. Now when it comes to me being a Father/Dad to my children, I did the best I could, and I wasn't away by choice, it was by force. I had to work to maintain a lifestyle you tried to uphold, hell, I was the only one working and with NO help. I hated being away from my children, but their mother did nothing to help me get back home. Did you ever try explaining that to them, how we would have had none of the things we had if it had not been for ME working. No but you would rather tell them I cheated on you and left you for another woman. I see what you are doing and all you want to do is make my name dirt to the girls, it hurts but time heals all wounds. I will be ok, in due time they will come around. Just make sure you let them know that you have had other priorities too ... Yeah, like not coming straight home in the evenings ... you seem to enjoy going out of your way after work to spend hours in and/or around Atlanta and another documented address before you go home at 8 to 10 at night ... There is a lot that you think I don't know, but trust and believe I know more than you think I know, but I would never tell the girls nor tell them anything to make them think that you are a "busy" woman ... IF you know what I mean :-) And my reply. No I am not proud but I again was tired and mad as hell.

To: Darren, April 18

Darren, Okay let us have this conversation because it is very obvious that you and Alexis (who I know wrote this email because it has too much b****a**ness, no real man has time to write all what she wrote) have many things confused. Now I was never going to have this conversation with you but it is apparent this is what you want. Now you talk about my family, let's talk about it really. Who after Sarah was born paid your bills because you could not afford to? MY MOMMA!! My same family who sent money to us in Germany and Texas when your ass could not afford to pay the bills. My same family who when we needed a deposit for the apartment and the earnest money for the Texas house sent over 5000.00 to make that happen. Let's talk about a leech, who was the one angry the time their father called asking for money? YOU!! Who was mad every time their sister called needing money whether it be for a bill or down payment on a vehicle? YOU!! Who kept saying why they always have their hands out? YOU!! For at least 10 years you complained about your family always having their hand in your pockets. You my love would always say, "why can't my family be like yours and not ask for any and never have their hand out." Let us not forget you asked if my dad could come here and take care of the kids because he gave up his plumbing business to do this, and at one point you were grateful. You also stated that I needed the help especially with our son having special needs and all the activities for the girls. You suggested the nanny!! Not me!!! Now you called me a Greedy, Money-Sucking Leech, how far from the truth. I was the chic who in the beginning when you did not have a dime would say, "It's okay, we will be okay."

THE MOMENT I DECIDED TO OWN IT

When you got demoted in rank due to again not being able to keep your hands to yourself and choking another solider and they took money out of our check, I was the one who said, "It's okay babe. I got you. We will be okay." When you went overseas, and I was working at the rental company, yes, you paid all the bills and took care of the home while my check went to the girls. Things like making sure you and the girls had Christmases with me receiving nothing but was okay with that because you all where happy. You were the one every time that came home and splurged on things that we did not need. You were the one paying your friend's rent, and helping out with college expenses for grown-ass women. I was the one who would say, "We don't need that," and you would say, "I worked hard to provide this and I want to do it." Let's not confuse roles about who spent money. I gave you a savings plan, and it worked but every time someone sold you a B.S. business, you blew it with nothing in return. By the way, you have that Hotel yet? CAN YOU TWO PLEASE STOP THINKING THERE IS MONEY STASHED!!! I begged you for years to come home, and you would say if you did we lose everything and you did not want to come back to make what you were making. YOUR daughters would say, "daddy we don't need this we want you." Sarah said she would have given up soccer just so you could be home like her other friends' dads. It was my friends' husbands picking up the girls and taking them out, NOT YOU!! You got accustom to making that money and did not want to let it go. Remember you handled your own money and however you mismanaged it was not my fault. You kept saying you could not make in the states with what you would earn. So please don't confuse who left who over there. What married fab single life, boo? I was at home doing what you failed to do. I was at home! I was raising OUR children. Sarah, the same child who YOU said you wash your hands of is graduating with 3.5 accepted into every school she applied to and you had nothing to do with it!! I have to come to the realization that I married your mother. How you ask? Because you did to my children what your mother did to you, walked away and blamed everyone else for leaving but not taking any responsibly for your actions. The difference between you and your mother was that she was sick, but you are just being you, BROKEN. A broken man is not equipped or capable to raise my strong boys into strong men. Now you are talking about trips. We only took two trips ever in our 19 years, and you were there both times. Now if you are talking about road trips with the girls, get your life together because every trip I took you knew, and it was never with your money but mine. Alexis if you are going to attempt to come for me, please be accurate with you information. Now please let me know what trips I took that you did not know about. Now, since you were concerned about my whereabouts these past few months let me address it. If you are talking about Atlanta, you know my aunt lives there. If you are talking about my personal life the girls know ALL about it, ask them they will tell you. They knew where I was at all times. Unlike you I have nothing to hide. Tell them, PLEASE tell them, and they will say, "Dad, we know." Heather will say, "Dad I know, because he comes to my soccer games and congratulated me on wins. He was the one who talked to me when I did not make varsity." Sarah will say, "He was the one who called before I went to prom and told me how beautiful I was." She will also say that he is the one who had that man to man talk with her boyfriend and explained how special she is and that he better not hurt her. And please, I was not as busy as you were during your lunch break at "camp." I know all about how you spent your "quickie" lunches. So please do not think I don't know what I know. Like you said, "What is wrong with having friends?" He was a friend who saw what I was dealing with in this divorce with a man who stopped taking care of his kids. Isn't that what your "friend" was to you?

Now let me address you, Alexis. You see, I never blamed you for the breakdown of my marriage because that was between Darren and I. I did not make you my focus in my divorce because at that point you were not that important, but because you keep putting yourself in my direct path, it is obvious you want my attention. So let me give it you. You told me last year that I needed a young woman to school my old behind. Well babe, let this old grown-behind woman schooling you. I know things as well. I know that married men are what you prefer since that last man you were involved with was also married but he did not leave his wife for you. I know that you advised Darren not to send any money to support his kids which got him in the situation he is in now with having to pay back child support and the huge amount he now owes to the mortgage company. Let me thank you for my monthly check. You did more for me than I could ever say, so let me say Thank you!!! Thank you from the bottom of my heart because without you, I could not be in the position I am in today. I also know that any real woman and mother would make sure that the man she was planning on marrying was taking care of his kids, but I am not dealing with a woman who has any worth. Now I have been very generous with my dealings with you because with all of the correspondence that I have between you and him would have affected your job and your money. Again, you were never my focus. But since you feel you can dictate how my money is handled please do not me let me start playing with yours. Let me have some emails, text messages, and correspondence come down the chain of command. Little girl please do not come for me unless I send for you, and I have not sent for you sweetie. Kindly stay in your place. Now enough of this tit for tat because I no longer have time to deal with or entertain this foolishness. We are no longer married so this pettiness is not worth my time. Do not be petty and please stay out of feelings and handle this payment. Kindly make sure that my child support and my first payment of the arrears is in my account today, unless you like paying both of our attorney's fees. All I need to know is did you send the payment because there are bills to be paid. Have a wonderful day.

I was not proud of my response but there comes a time when you have put your foot down and say what needs to be said. For far too long I allowed Darren to say and do what he wanted to do and kept quiet, but there comes a time when enough is enough. I had to let go and say what needed to be said.

Advice to my former self, my daughters, and you, my readers: Always remember even in your darkest hour you are not alone. There will be times that you feel that no one cares and that you are left here to battle this fight by yourself, but you are not. These moments come to define your faith, strength, and resilience. There will be times some minor battles will be lost but when you have truth on your side you will always win the war. Remember it takes fire to make steel.

CHAPTER ELEVEN:
I'M LOST

THERE WERE TIMES during the divorce process that I thought I was in this by myself; I felt as though God wanted me to suffer. I thought that He had turned his back on me and I was so angry. At times I could not and would not pray. In March 2014, when we went to mediation and in my mind I said okay, today will be the final day and I will be done, I was wrong! I remember during mediation all I could think was, *He is lying,* and wanted to scream that to everyone. He told his attorney he lost his job and that is why he had not paid child support for three months or the mortgage that he was court-ordered to pay, that his contract was amended and that he was making less money. He suggested that he reduce his child support, that I assume the mortgage in my name in two months, and that I also be awarded the other property we had in Texas. I remember at one point during the mediation process the statement was made "Why don't you give him custody of the kids, so he can see what it is like?"

I became angry and said, "I would rather work three jobs and live in a two-bedroom apartment than to ever give up my children."

After our mediation I was angry. I was mad as hell, and on the brink of snapping. I was tired, and tired of feeling like this man was getting away with everything. He thought he could do whatever he wanted, and I called a close friend of mine, screaming in the phone about what happened. I told her that even though all I had left was $250 to last me for the week and he had just gotten paid that day, I had to help pay half of the session and it took every penny I had left and he had no worries.

She said to me, "What do you want me to do? Tell me, and I will do it." I was so angry in that moment, I told her if I could I would have run him over in the parking lot. In that moment I could see how women ended up in jail in situations like this. After that failed mediation, he went back to spend the rest of the week with his fiancée and did not even ask to see his children. You see, every time he came for a court visit, seeing his children was not on the top of his to-do list, and every time I had to be the one to wipe the tears from my oldest daughters' faces. I then promised myself that I would not allow him to continue to hurt my children. I looked every one of my children in the eyes and vowed to be the parent that they could always depend on.

You see, I have learned in this process that many times the absentee parent divorces not only the spouse but the children, and will turn around and blame the spouse for the lack of relationship with the children instead of taking responsibility for their own actions. I have oftentimes said that it is always easier to place blame on another person than take ownership of your own wrongs. But what I did for my children throughout this was learn the art of forgiveness. I do not say that lightly because it was not an easy road. When I saw the hurt my children were going through I had to release my own anger and pain in order for them to do the same. Then one day I did something I never thought I could do: I prayed for him. I prayed that God would continue to bless him and keep him. Now, at first, I kept it real with God, and I said, "Now, God, this is hard for me but I know in order for You to bless me I have to be able to pray and love my enemies, so Father, watch over him and keep him safe from harm and danger; bless him as You have continued to bless me."

And no sooner did I pray that prayer for him, I received notice that the home that he was supposed to get the payments caught up on was going into foreclosure. You see, that is how the devil works to keep you off your focus, and all I could do at the moment was breathe.

During the months that lead to the final divorce hearing, I had to do some inner reflecting and soul searching to really understand how I allowed this in my life. I had to figure out what within me was lacking that I could allow anyone to treat me like this. You see it is always easier to look at other people's situation and judge it, but it is not that easy to turn the spotlight on yourself. I had to do it because I believe without really digging within myself, I would repeat this same situation again. The only difference, his name would be different, but ultimately I would find myself looking in the mirror again at loneliness, heartbreak, and pain staring back at me. It was now time to uncover some ugly truths about me that I tucked away from everyone, including myself. I had to go back to the beginning—the beginning before there was a marriage, divorce, and five children. Until the age of 13, my childhood was no different than most. I played, had friends, but for some reason always felt less adequate than everyone else. I would do more to seek attention, always looking for affirmation from anyone. Lacking the self-confidence that I instilled in my own children, I always thought that everyone else was prettier than me, smarter than me. Watching those around me excel, I oftentimes felt as if I had to do more to be accepted. At the age of 13, my perception of the world changed. The childhood my parents dreamt for me was stolen in a single moment.

You see, at the age of 13 I was molested and the Tanya that was once died. I was molested, not by a stranger or someone I did not know. I was molested three times by a family member. I kept this secret for two years, believing that this is what I brought on myself. Thinking that if I had listened to my parents about not being so overly friendly, this would not have happened to me. During the time I was holding tight to this secret I started to self-destruct. I would lie for no reason. I wanted more attention from boys. I would not do the things that my parents asked of me. I had gotten to the point that I would have no regards for anything or anyone, including myself. The night that I told my family what I thought would have occurred did not. There were no hugs, tears, or I am sorry. Not even the most important words, "Tanya, I believe you."

What I did hear was "Do not tell anyone," as if I was the family's shame and not his. In my mind, I assumed they thought I was lying about this like I did with other things. For about a week there was no conversation with me or around me. It was like I was nonexistent. Feeling more alone than ever, I thought to myself I was better off keeping this secret. Some of my family just did not believe me. I felt ostracized by the people who I thought loved me. I remember overhearing a phone call that went like this: "Well, Tanya said she was molested and so we have to go to New Jersey to figure this out."

I stood outside of the kitchen where the phone call took place and felt again alone. No one will truly understand how I felt the day that my parents, sister, and I drove from Florida to New Jersey to have this "family confrontation." When we got there, I was a 15-year-old girl having to defend herself to her family in front of her rapist—who sat there drunk. Sitting there in that chair having to replay each instance in front of everyone in that room made the 13-year-old girl trapped inside want to scream.

To my left was one side of my family that I knew believed me and to my right were the eyes of those I knew did not believe me. In that moment in a room full of "family" I was alone. Nothing else came from that moment; it is something that was not truly spoken of, even to this day. That one moment forever changed the course of my life, and the relationships that I had with men. All of my relationships were flawed, and I allowed it to happen. When I started as a freshman in high school, I dated John, who was abusive in every form of the word. Our relationship did not start that way. It was great until the day John saw me talking to a male friend of his. I will never forget that day. John confronted me in the hallway at school for talking to him, and the conversation quickly went from him grabbing me by the throat and telling me that if that happened again he would kill me. This scenario happened a few times until I said that enough is enough. Then shortly after that relationship I dated David for almost four years. While everyone at the time could see how controlling he was, I did not. I simply thought it was love. If David had told me to jump I would have asked how high. It wasn't until years later that I learned the difference.

During that time in our relationship my parents really did not approve of it, and I would sneak around just to see him and pay the consequences for my actions later. But I did not care; I did not want to lose him. David at the time was my world I remember that shortly after he broke up with me the second time, I started talking to a wonderful guy named Carl, and David said to me, "I just don't like the fact someone else gets to enjoy all the hard work I put into you."

I shook my head and laughed, thinking, *What hard work? Was I a project that had to be fixed?*

Actually I did need to be fixed but no man could have done it.

I dated a guy who truly cared about me and he showed me what unconditional love was, but I was too damaged to appreciate it. Shortly after graduation Carl and I broke up. I was going off to college, and he still had one more year of high school. I left to go off to college in New Jersey, and I was simply a train wreck waiting to happen. I then met Arron, who was truly wonderful to me. He was working hard for his education and had his goals set, but again, I was not ready to believe that someone cared about me like that and I also destroyed that relationship. I started dating men who simply used me. It had gotten to the point that I received a phone call from home about my embarrassing behavior and how recklessly I was treating my life. At that point I did not care about my life. It was true, I was not focused on school anymore; I was too busy partying and filling my time with things that did not matter. I reconnected with an old friend, Alex, from my childhood and I started seeing the potential in a wonderful relationship with him but as soon as it got really serious I literally jumped on the plane back to Florida. Afraid that he would see the damaged young woman I was. *Who could truly love me?* was all I thought. I left without even a goodbye.

When I got back to Florida, I met a football player named Eric at the university and it moved fast, way too fast, and one day after a night at the club with my friends we had a full blowout fight. It went from accusations to being pinned on the bed fighting. When I left his room, I thought to myself that this was not what I do. I refused to be in any relationship where the only way to handle a conflict was to put your hands on me. It only took one time and I was done. When I left his room our relationship was over. Before I had time to work on me, I met Darren, and that is how I allowed him to walk in and stay for so long. I firmly believe that while he was broken, so was I, and two broken people are not made whole when you put them together. You are just two pieces of a half that are not good for each other, and we were not good for one another.

Advice to my former self, my daughters, and to you, my readers: Never get stuck in a moment. Take from it all the lessons that it has taught you, but move on from it. Cry, scream, get angry, have your moments, but keep living, keep moving, and keep pressing forward. When you hold yourself bound to a moment, you keep yourself stuck in a place that was only meant to be a learning experience. In life we will have life-changing moments, but we must make a daily decision not to stay in that place of hurt, fear, bitterness, and disappointment. Every single day we must make the choice to keep living. I chose to live past my moment. You see, if we stay in the past we will not be prepared for all the blessings that life continues to bring.

CHAPTER TWELVE:

DIGGING DEEP

MANY PEOPLE MAY WONDER why I stayed for so long, but to be honest, I stayed for my own selfish reasons. I was afraid to be on my own. I was afraid of change. I thought that nobody else would love me through all my flaws and I came with much baggage. Like so many other women, I simply stayed until I had no choice but to move on. To be honest, my marriage never truly had a chance because I was damaged and so was he. During the time of my loneliness, while going through my divorce, it was extremely difficult to be around other couples. I did not want to hear about what they were doing with their families because my family unit was broken. I did not want to hear about family vacations, surprise birthday parties, or anything family related. I was jealous; I wanted what they had. I envied them, and I wanted the happily ever after that was in my head.

My married friends thought that I had just become reclusive, but that truly was not the case. I just could not be around them. The pain was too much at times. I had to deal with the death of my own marriage, and I could not truly be happy for anyone else even when I tried, so I just stayed away. I did not want to become that friend who was always complaining about the issues in my life. I didn't want to bring other people down with my own personal issues, and I never wanted anyone to ever feel that every time I called it was due to issues I was having with my soon to be ex-husband. The wonderful thing about all of this is that the women that God placed in my life never once complained about my venting. They never said, "Tanya, I don't want to hear it," and they made themselves available when I needed them the most. Never being too busy, each one showed up and showed out!

Advice to my former self, my daughters, and to you, my readers: Always surround yourself with women who not only listen to you but will also pray for you. Women who will be strong for you when you cannot be strong for yourself! God will always have the right people in your life.

In conclusion, I learned a lot of things about myself. Some pretty and some not so pretty. The months after he left was the first time in my entire adult life I was by myself. I learned that staying does not make you stronger. Walking away from what is not meant for you is what shows how truly strong you are. Many times we as women stay, thinking that this is making us stronger, and it will all work out in the end. I heard the following statement, which was so accurate: "So many times we hold on to the very thing that God is trying to take away from us so that he can make way for our greater blessing."

Oftentimes we as women think that "it isn't all bad, it could be worse, hell at least he is not beating me or cheating on me." What a horrible way to live. Now, again, it is not easy, ending any relationship, whether it be a marriage or even a friendship, but you have to look beyond that right now and try to see how much more fulfilling life can be. I had to discover who I actually was. I was more than a wife, or now ex-wife. I was more than a mother, a cook, a counselor, a personal driver, a cheerleader, a housekeeper, and at times a father. I was, and continue to be, a woman, a fighter, and always an overcomer!

There were so many times during this process that life could have taken me out, but each time I dug my feet in a little deeper because I refused to let go. I had and still have five people who depend on me, my children. I wanted to make sure that my children, especially Sarah, Heather, and Tiffany, know that life might knock you down, but I don't raise quitters. I had to live the life I expected of them. I taught them that life is not fair, but you do not use that as an excuse. If I expected that of them, I had to step up to the plate and walk this thing out. Now, I've had some falls and tumbles, but like any great fighter I've gotten back up. I remember times that I would play my theme songs: one by Whitney Houston—"I Didn't Know My Own Strength"—and the other by Destiny's Child—"Survivor." These songs empowered me on my difficult days.

You see, I refused to lose the war. I may have lost some battles, but I was not going to lose the war. One of the major things I learned was that no matter how powerful it may be, the love of a good woman will not change the heart of the wrong man! We as women need to stop looking for a man and let the right man find you! I am not perfect. By the time you read this, I will have fallen a thousand more times, but the one thing I know is my Bible and it gives great references to strong women, and one of them is Ruth. I look at Ruth, who after she lost her husband, followed her mother-in-law Naomi back to her hometown and said, "Where you go I will go ... Your people will be my people and your God my God" (Ruth 1:16). You see, Ruth wasn't looking for a husband because she was looking for God. And one day while she was where God wanted her to be, gleaning in the fields, her future husband, Boaz, found her. I know that is easier said than done. I know what it is like to go to bed alone and all you are wanting is someone to hold you while you sleep.

But let me say this: I would rather go to sleep by myself than with a devil in my bed. I just put one out, and I refuse to put another there just to say I have someone. Wait on God to bring the right person because doing it on your own will bring the same devil and the same confusion. Always remember this—God will never bring you someone else's husband! If they show up, send them back. I do not care how you try to justify it by saying things such as, "He is just not happy in his marriage" or "His wife does not love him" or "God sent us to each other." No, God did not bring you together; loneliness and selfishness did. God will not bless that union. What God has for you will not come with a ring on the left ring finger, even if they choose not to wear it. When you do not allow God and time to restore the heart of who you are, you will fall into the same situation again, if not worse. It may come in a different name and even packaging, but the outcome is still the same.

It never made sense to me to jump out of the fire and into the frying pan. My advice to anyone is to take time to heal before you enter into another relationship. Make sure that your heart is receptive to what God has for you. The older I get, the more I realize my tolerance for foolishness diminishes, and I refuse to allow history to repeat itself again in my life. The process that I went through was not easy, and not everyone is able to walk this road, but trust in God to know that He will put you on a path that even at your breaking point He will carry you through. There were days that I would get up a little earlier and put on my "face" so when my kids woke up, I could put on a brave smile as if all was well with the world while on the inside I was dying. I would have never known the person I am today if I had not gone through the storm and the rain. I stand firm and say in order to help someone who is struggling with something you have to have gone through it yourself. I may have had a ton of losses and lots of sleepless nights—but I survived.

There were days that I would be driving down the street and the tears would flow without explanation. A song would play on the radio and memories of happier times would flood my mind, because even though we had some bad times we also had good moments. I would say, "Maybe if I had been different ... " but the truth was that it would not have mattered. Our journey is complete and I know it. I have shed my river of tears, but I rejoice in the woman I am now because of it. I am Tanya Renee: I am not only a mother, a former wife, a sister, a daughter, a niece, a granddaughter, and a friend, but I am an overcomer, a survivor, and a Child of God!

CHAPTER THIRTEEN:
THE AHA MOMENT

WHILE IT WOULD BE SO EASY to blame my ex-husband about many things, and I mean many things, the truth of the matter is I allowed it. It is always easier to blame everyone else around you so that you do not have to take inventory of your own self. Now, trust me when I say that it is not easy to really check yourself, but if you do not you will forever keep making the same faulty decisions over again—just with different people.

You see, I could have written a book about all the wrongs of Darren and made it seem that I was perfect, but I would have been disingenuous not only to you the reader but to myself. I want healing for you the reader, but I needed healing for me. I had to take some real hard looks at myself and see my faults and my mistakes. When I truly began to take inventory and ownership of all my issues I did not like what I was seeing in myself.

I would have been held prisoner to my past if I did not turn around and look into the mirror and see my naked self. Well, let me tell you, honey, I saw some things that I had to admit about myself, but you see, I refuse to walk down this path again, so I had to look at the good, the bad, and yes, Lawd, the ugly. You see, while driving in my car talking with my publicist/manager, I had my "Own It Moment."

I had to own the fact that I married a liar because I was a liar. I had to own that I married a cheater because I had cheated in previous relationships. I had to own that I was married to a man who could not handle money because I could not handle money. I had to own that I married a man with bad credit because, hell, I had bad credit. I had to own that I married a man who was broken because I was broken. I had to own that I was lonely and always had to have someone in my life. I had to own that I was always seeking attention and approval from others. I had to own that at times I was not a good friend to those who were great friends to me. I had to own that I was selfish and always wanted things to go my way without looking for ways to compromise. I had to own my insecurities. I had to own that I at times was envious of my friends. I had to own some things, and, listen, it is not easy to admit that, but I understand now that in order to be free to walk into my destiny I had to own my past.

Once I owned that thang, honey, I was free from it. Now listen! If you want better for yourself, let me give you a Tanyaism:

THE MOMENT I DECIDED TO OWN IT

You better own that thang, honey, embrace it, boo, honor it and let it go!

You see, once you own it, you will understand it, and you will not allow it to happen to you again. I had to own the woman I once was so I could prepare the woman who is here today! Listen, I am so not ashamed of that old person, because without her, I would not be me, and I am so proud of me today. As I thought more about the own it chapter, I went further and looked up the true definition of "own," and this is what I found:

- Of or belonging to oneself or itself
- To admit or acknowledge that something is the case or that one feels a certain way
- Synonyms: admit, concede, grant, accept, acknowledge, agree, confess

You see, when you own your faults, you free yourself from what others can say about you. There will be nothing about you that can be said, because you acknowledged your mistakes and that frees you from the opinions, judgment, and condemnation of others.

If someone chooses to remind you of the things you owned and let go of, then you can cock your head to the left, place your hand on your hip, and say, "And your point is what?" Please understand, a person cannot hold anything over you that you took ownership of. My ex-husband can right now tell me you lied to me during our marriage (which I did), you were bad with money (which I was), you had bad credit (which I did), you had insecurities (which I did), you had a bad attitude and held grudges (which I did), you did not love me like a wife should love her husband (which I did not), you were selfish (which I was), you never compromised and always wanted things your own way (which I did), you were disrespectful toward me (which I was), and my response last year would have been "No, that is not true. I was none of those things." But my response today is "I know that, and your point is? Come at me with something I didn't own." Do you see the difference in the two responses? The former me would have tried to hide the flaws and imperfections, but the me of today takes full ownership and, with much Tanya attitude, embraces it.

Allow yourself the opportunity to walk in your total freedom with no shame guilt or remorse. For the women who are going through this season in your life, here is my "put on your grown woman panties" advice: Fight! Stop crying and fight! Fight for your joy, fight for your happiness, fight for your peace, and fight for your children and for yourself.

When I was backed up against the wall I fought. I fought like hell. I dug my feet in deeper and I stood my ground. I was no longer playing the victim in my own life. I was not going to play that part any longer. I know when I was coming through this thing called divorce that God had bigger plans for me. I had to go through this storm; I had to lose to gain more than I could have imaged for myself. During this process I had real conversations with God, and I remember saying, "Take one more thing! I can't lose anything else! I can't carry another load! What have I done in my life to deserve this kind of pain?"

After coming through this journey, I now know that I can do it! It's when you lose what you thought you needed that God will show you your true strength. There are times that He has to pull people and things away from you that will not take you to the places He is trying to get you to go. Repeat these words: "I am stronger than this. I am stronger than the person who left me. I am stronger than this pain. I am stronger than the hurt. I am stronger than what I thought I needed. I will survive because weeping may endure for a night, but joy, true joy, comes in the morning. I thank you for strength!"

You see, when you truly let go of the very thing or person you thought you needed, what you truly need will show up, but you have to be ready. When they do, you will know. I have had many "get over it" experiences. I can say this: shed your tears, have your bad days, ask your questions, but then get over it! There is a purpose in your pain. Your marriage ended, your relationship ended, but not your life. Keep living, keep moving, keep fighting, and always keep God first. You will survive! Remember the words that I said every day for the first six months: "I just have to get through today to get to tomorrow."

You can get through today! This is the reason I now have faith, family, freedom, and my children. The moment you realize how great life can be ... that's the moment you own it!

TANYA ARMSTRONG is the mother of five beautiful children. She is a divorce survivor that prides herself on mentoring and coaching other women that have gone through similar situations and want to "OWN It" and get back on track in their lives.

www.ingramcontent.com/pod-product-compliance
Lightning Source LLC
Chambersburg PA
CBHW051657040426
42446CB00009B/1176